D1517292

# INSIDE TIPS

## *A Transformation Workbook*

### SWAMI PARAMESHWARANANDA

**BALBOA**
PRESS

A DIVISION OF HAY HOUSE

Copyright © 2011 *Swami Parameshwarananda.*

All rights reserved. No part of this book may be used or reproduced by any means, graphic, electronic, or mechanical, including photocopying, recording, taping or by any information storage retrieval system without the written permission of the publisher except in the case of brief quotations embodied in critical articles and reviews.

ISBN: 978-1-4525-3761-0 (sc)
ISBN: 978-1-4525-3760-3 (e)

Balboa Press books may be ordered through booksellers or by contacting:

Balboa Press
A Division of Hay House
1663 Liberty Drive
Bloomington, IN 47403
www.balboapress.com
1-(877) 407-4847

Because of the dynamic nature of the Internet, any web addresses or links contained in this book may have changed since publication and may no longer be valid. The views expressed in this work are solely those of the author and do not necessarily reflect the views of the publisher, and the publisher hereby disclaims any responsibility for them.

The author of this book does not dispense medical advice or prescribe the use of any technique as a form of treatment for physical, emotional, or medical problems without the advice of a physician, either directly or indirectly. The intent of the author is only to offer information of a general nature to help you in your quest for emotional and spiritual well-being. In the event you use any of the information in this book for yourself, which is your constitutional right, the author and the publisher assume no responsibility for your actions.

Any people depicted in stock imagery provided by Thinkstock are models, and such images are being used for illustrative purposes only.

Certain stock imagery © Thinkstock.

Printed in the United States of America

Balboa Press rev. date: 9/06/2011

# CONTENTS

# INTRODUCTION

So why are we alive? One answer is to realize who we really are. And who are we? That's a question that can last us a lifetime. Let's tackle it anyway.

We have an inner essence, a truth within us. This essence is love. This truth is that we're not the body, we're much more. We're limitless. We're soul, Self, a divine presence that's waiting to be revealed to us and expressed in our lives. How do the revelation and expression happen? Through our own focus, discipline, and decisions to transform.

Yes, this is spiritual talk because it's about Spirit. Since you've picked up this book, and you know it's by a swami, I assume this kind of talk is your cup of tea. If it isn't, it may be time to close the book.

Back to this inner essence; it's eternal, powerful beyond our imaginations, and meant to be manifested through our thoughts, feelings, words, and actions. It's our birthright to live as this Spirit in every moment of our lives. We're in a physical body for this reason: to live this, be this, serve as this so others come to the same realization and express who they truly are.

This book is a means toward that end. It gives you a structure, format, and tools that guide you through the journey of self-transformation so you realize your essence, your truth, and live it powerfully each day. Now what about this title, *Inside Tips: A Transformation Workbook*?

**Inside Tips**. This workbook provides tips, or pointers, based on powerful lessons I've learned since I consciously began my spiritual path over sixteen years ago. This has been a time of great blessing because I've spent it with my beloved guru, Her Holiness Sai Maa Lakshmi Devi. I couldn't have written this book without Maa's teachings, love, and service to myself and so many others. This book comes from my devotion to and my experiences with Maa. You're not obliged to have Maa as your guru, or any guru. In going through this book, just know how powerful the tips are, the wisdom they're based on, and the accelerated transformation that has taken place in me and others through Maa's grace and guidance.

The tips point you in a direction I know will serve you in your transformation because they have served me. I'm not unique; we have much in common. I've suffered, and these tips will reduce your suffering. I've evolved, and these tips will serve your evolution. They're inside tips because they come from someone who has been on the inside of what it's like to transform, of what serves in the spiritual path. In addition, they're inside tips because of a very important teaching: *everything's inside of us.* We don't have to go anywhere else to find what we're looking for in our lives. We can stop playing hide-and-go-seek, where we hide from ourselves and seek other people or things to fulfill us.

**Transformation**. Change is about taking something and changing how it looks, creating a different form of the same thing like re-plastering or painting walls. Transformation is about creating a completely new form that didn't exist before. It's about invention and creation, transforming something so you can't trace back to its original form.

In this case, we're speaking about *your* transformation; transforming your thoughts and feelings, how you see yourself and the world, how you feel about yourself and the world; transforming your words and actions; how you communicate, how you relate to others, how you express yourself each day. Fundamentally, the work and this book are about transforming who you are, who you're being in the world, and what you're creating and manifesting in your life.

**Workbook**. Like other workbooks, this one has some tables, diagrams and forms, lists, and categories of questions and practices that will assist you. Is it "work"? Well, it doesn't have to be work, meaning difficult and an effort. It's Work with a capital "w," in the sense of doing the work—the work of transformation. It can be joyful, dynamic, creative, and life affirming. It's up to you how you approach it and what you commit to in doing the work.

In summary, this book provides questions and practices that support you in going inside and finding the wealth of wisdom, the breadth of qualities and dimensions you are in truth. This book assists you in doing the work of transformation, using the pointers, structure, and tools to realize what's inside of you, and to reinvent yourself so you live and serve as this in the world.

# THE TRANSFORMATIONAL JOURNEY

Here are two important questions to start off:

In taking this journey, it's important you answer this question: *"How do I relate to my own transformation?"* Are you open, willing, and committed? Are you confident or uncertain? Are you thinking about your gifts and talents or your weaknesses and shortcomings? Are you in it for the short haul or long haul? Take a little time to inquire into yourself about this. It's your relationship right now, and it's also an ongoing question as you take the journey in each moment.

A second question: *"What's my vision of myself after having made this transformation?"* This means, who are you being? How are you thinking, feeling, and acting? How are you showing up in the world? How are you expressing yourself? This isn't about expectations with specific measures and standards. This is about your overall vision or picture of yourself through your transformation. Keep in mind that the time it takes for your vision to manifest depends upon your answer to the first question.

Now take a look at Diagram 1 on page 4. It's a depiction of your transformational journey using the tools provided in this workbook. It's the perspective and approach we're all taking on this journey together.

We start with transformation itself. Our transformation is a movement like ripples in the water that keep expanding out more and more with greater impact. Our transformation impacts deeper and deeper aspects of ourselves, and an increasing number of people and circumstances in our lives. Let's take this to an even higher level. Our transformation creates waves of energy—an energetic field of impact—through who we're being and how we're acting that contribute to the transformation of the planet.

Another analogy is that we're the river, and through our transformation we join and become the ocean. This isn't about water; it's about merging in the ocean of Self. We realize and express our true Self more as we transform. Finally, we become one with Self and live as this in the world. Our journey is about movement, expansion, impact, and union.

Next, let's focus on *self-inquiry*. When we ask ourselves questions and reflect about our answers, we become more aware. We're more aware of ourselves, our states and inner lives. We're more aware of how we view the world and approach life, and how this impacts us and our lives. We're more aware of our thoughts and emotions, and how we communicate and relate. In sum, we understand more what's working and not working, and what needs to transform in us.

Then there are *practices*. Practices are those actions we take within ourselves and with others that lead to our transformations. We can also call these spiritual practices because they lead us to express Spirit in physical form, to live as this in the world. In Sanskrit, the word is *sadhana* or daily spiritual practice. These practices reflect where we're focusing our transformation, and carrying them out reflects our decisions and commitments to transform.

As this diagram shows, self-inquiry is central and core to the practices, while also being a practice in itself. We're carrying out the practice of self-inquiry when we ask ourselves questions, come up with answers, and become more aware. When we're more aware of what we're to transform through our reflection, we can choose specific practices to transform in those areas. We know the "what" and can more readily choose the "how." Thus, self-inquiry serves two purposes: it directs us to other practices, and it transforms us itself through increased self-awareness.

# THE TRANSFORMATIONAL JOURNEY

Finally, there's the *action plan*. You can see this is at the base of the journey, because the plan serves as a strong, solid foundation on which the practices are carried out and our transformations stay on course. This doesn't mean that each practice has to be specified in a written action plan. It just means that the plan serves to provide focus and structure for carrying out certain practices. In writing down the actions, we feel everything is more manageable; our transformation doesn't feel as overwhelming or undoable. We can also hold a plan in our minds as we take action.

Even though the action plan provides structure, it doesn't mean the plan is rigid or limited. It provides an approach and parameters within which we act, a way for us to be disciplined. When you look at the actual plan format, you'll see that the plan is an agreement and commitment you make with yourself and with others who are involved. It's a declaration of your intention to transform in certain areas.

Let's put it all together now. You ask yourself questions, answer them, and become more aware. This awareness informs you about where you need to transform, and the choices you'll make about practices for transforming in those areas. In addition, the awareness transforms you. The action plan provides you with a framework for making agreements about how you'll carry out certain practices.

This journey of transformation is a living process, where self-inquiry and new awareness lead to practices and transformation. In turn, that transformation leads to new awareness, renewed self-inquiry, new practices, and so forth. The components are interrelated and continuous in our lives as we progress in the spiritual path, as we take the journey to realizing ourselves and living powerfully in the world.

## Use of the Workbook

What follows are the structure and tools for you to learn about yourself, the identify you'd like to transform, choosing specific practices for your transformation, and establishing a plan or agreement for how you'll go about transforming. The process of your transformation is laid out in four steps with associated materials: (1) inquiring into yourself using specific questions for reflection; (2) identifying practice areas of focus for your transformation; (3) choosing top priority practices in those areas; (4) creating an action plan.

### Step 1: Asking the Questions (Self-Inquiry)

In this step, you ask yourself questions using those that are included in Appendix 1. Of course, you're *not* restricted to just using these questions. Ask yourself whatever you need to in order to become more aware of yourself and where you're to transform in your life.

The questions are organized into themes, which are shown in Table 1 on page 7, Framework for Awareness and Action. Step 1 is about awareness. Let's go through the different themes so you have a sense of where to concentrate your inner reflection. This will give you the lay of the land on which you'll create your path for transformation.

**Self-Awareness** includes those questions that are more inner-directed. You ask yourself these questions to get a better sense of what's going on inside of you, how you see yourself, your state, aspects and dimensions of yourself, your energy, openness, willingness, commitments, and responses to change and transition.

**Perspectives about Life and the World** includes questions that are more outer-directed, meaning your views of what's out there, such as possibilities, abundance, and miracles. Questions also focus on your views about time, ancestors and lineage, past life experiences, religion and spirituality, and gurus.

**Focus and Attention** enables you to be more aware of where you place your attention, what you value. Areas include outside goals or inner values, inner or outer life, heart or mind, past, present or future, feminine or masculine sides of yourself. Questions also cover the ego and its influence on where you focus, including doubt, attachments, daily distractions, and fantasies.

**Emotions** questions bring you greater awareness about your fears, moods, worries, judgments, needs for control and being right, emotion-based ailments, as well as your mastery in shifting these emotions and states.

**Relationships** questions bring you greater clarity about love and compassion, listening and expressing yourself, aspects of your close relationships with partners, children, other family members, and friends. The questions also cover your relationships with community and with those you lead.

**Sadhana/Spiritual Practices** contains questions pertaining to the actual practices you have in your life to transform, and your overall approach to your practices, meaning devotion, joy, doing or being. You'll learn about how you view or carry out specific practices, including breathing, meditation, reciting mantras, chanting, movement, exercise, nutrition, rest and relaxation, and selfless service.

TABLE 1:
# Framework for Awareness and Action

| Self-Inquiry<br>(Themes) | Practices<br>(Areas of Focus) |
| --- | --- |
| **Self-Awareness**<br>• Sense of self/inner state<br>• Approach to living life<br>• Commitment<br>• Personal changes and evolution<br>• Energy | **Inner State**<br>Creating or shifting your state |
| **Perspectives About Life and the World**<br>• View of what life offers<br>• Sense of time and life experience<br>• Spirituality | **Energy (within yourself, with others)**<br>Accessing, using and transforming energy |
| **Focus and Attention**<br>• Internal/external<br>• Heart/mind<br>• Broad/narrow and time focus<br>• Distractions and ego<br>• Feminine/masculine | **Thoughts**<br>Gaining new awareness for action, shifting and transforming thoughts |
| **Emotions**<br>• Fears<br>• Worrying<br>• Mastering moods and emotions<br>• Judgment/control/ego<br>• Physical impact | **Emotions and Fears**<br>Releasing and transforming them |
| **Relationships**<br>• Love/compassion/communication<br>• Close relationships<br>• Community/diversity<br>• Leadership | **Self-Expression**<br>Communicating and expressing yourself in new ways, a new way of being |
| **Sadhana/Spiritual Practices** | **Relationships**<br>Transforming them with family, friends, colleagues, community |
|  | **Health**<br>Being more aware of, strengthening your health |

Review the themes in Table 1 with their associated topics. Then go to Appendix 1 and review the questions. Read them over to get a feeling for the types of questions in each theme, and if any interest you right away, spend more time looking at these.

In approaching the questions, there are at least three ways you can use them to pinpoint where you're to focus your transformation. These ways also apply to any questions you come up with by yourself that will serve your self-inquiry.

First, choose one or more questions based on what you already know about yourself, and then sit and reflect. Lie in bed in the morning or at night and contemplate. Go for a walk in nature. Sit at your altar. Pick up this book regularly and see what questions are pertinent at different points in time.

Second, journal. This is a very important and beneficial practice in and of itself. Buy a journal that suits you. Use it to note down answers to specific questions that feel very pertinent to what's going on within you or in your life. You might have a sense of what's not working, or where you might need to concentrate your transformation. In this case, choose the related questions, write, and reflect. When you write, new questions will come to mind that you can answer by writing or just reflecting again. Reflecting and journaling will direct you to other questions listed in the workbook.

In addition, journal any thoughts and feelings that come to you during the day. Note what's happened, your perspective about it, what you're learning about yourself and your relationships. Use the journal to highlight and reflect about your *sadhana* or spiritual practice, what you're doing and how it affects you. Specify the benefits or any concerns about your practices, successes, and where you need to focus more to transform.

Third, have conversations with others focusing on specific questions. Talk to others who are important in your life using questions that are of particular significance at the moment. Express yourself honestly and authentically to the other person. Listen generously to what others have to say. See how your answers impact your relationships and help you to be more aware of what you need to transform. Use the questions in conversations with your community, in group settings, during *satsang* or spiritual gatherings. Choose certain themes with associated questions for a daylong conversation, or for a theme of the month with your group.

Once you've used these questions in conversations within yourself or with others, you should be more aware of where you're to focus your transformation.

**Illustrative Example: Will Powers**

We'll use an example running through all the steps. Let's call this person Will Powers.

Will is conflicted about whether he's committed to a certain cause; in his case enrolling his organization, coworkers, and local community in cleaning up the neighborhood, including creating several community gardens. He asks himself questions under Commitment within Self-Awareness. He realizes through his reflection and journaling that he's actually very committed to the cause. He just wants to inspire himself more, do something within himself to be more powerful in taking action. We'll come back to Will in the next step.

## Step 2: Choosing the Focus for Your Practice

The information you've collected during Step 1 serves as the foundation for identifying the area of focus for the practices you'll choose to transform. Although there may be more than one area of focus, begin with what you feel is the most important relative to your immediate transformation. Again, this means transformation that will lead you to be powerful and self-expressive in the world. When you transform, you'll be free of any perspectives, thoughts, or emotions that limit you. You'll be demonstrating healthier relationships. In other words, you'll be living more as Spirit in your daily life.

In this step, you'll choose among seven areas of focus within which you'll identify specific practices in Step 3.

### Understanding the practice areas

Let's go through all the areas of focus so you understand them more.

Tables 1 and 2 describe each area of focus. Begin with Table 1 and go down the right-hand column of practices (areas of focus) with the corresponding definitions in each box. The areas are: Inner State, Energy, Thoughts, Emotions and Fears, Self-Expression, Relationships and Health.

After you have a general feel for the seven areas, go to the top and begin with Inner State. These practices enable you to create or shift your state. Now go to Table 2 and look at the specific practices within Inner State so you get an even better sense of this area of focus. They include going within, breathing, expressing love, gratitude, and joy, reciting mantras, affirmations, uniting heart and mind, and feminine and masculine. You'll use Appendix 2 later in Step 3 to review the practices in more detail so you can choose which to pursue.

# TABLE 2:
## Practices within Areas of Focus

### Inner State

Breathe, slow down with the breath; reallocate your time and go within; practice *"Nowism"*; meditate; create a sacred space; use the centering technique; be grateful; develop more love for yourself; laugh and be joyful; practice affirmations with "I AM"; recite mantras; unite the Divine Masculine and Feminine (Sri Chakra); develop the relationship of mind and heart; radiate coherence.

### Energy

#### Within yourself

Use your energy; relate to your energy; see your light; play with your energy; manifest your intention; embody your master; manifest a master; use the Brain Illumination Method.

#### With others

Transform group energy; choose the energies you're in; don't be affected by energies; practice *Sai Maa Diksha*.

### Thoughts

Think in the body; move thoughts from the mind to the heart; stick out your tongue; reduce your processing time; create a powerful context for yourself; drop expectations; shift your relationship with making mistakes; master your focus; unattach yourself; stop resisting; review lost opportunities; reduce and benefit from your fantasy life.

### Emotions and Fears

Transform the emotion by bringing it to your heart; transform the emotion by spreading light within it; use the release method; transform the triggers; be a witness to your reactions and emotions; stop criticizing yourself; face and transform your worries; eliminate doubt.

### Self-Expression

Shift from automatic to authentic listening; practice authentic expression; feed devotion not doubt; be your truth; speak up; go with what feels right; say "yes" more often; identify the fit and pursue necessary life changes; we're creators so create; apply lessons; simplify; serve however you can; experiment with your feminine side; balance your masculine and feminine sides; express yourself as a leader.

### Relationships

Communicate; find ways to express your love and gratitude; check in; experiment with the keys to a divine relationship; show more of yourself; do practices together in your relationship; clean up your relationships; express forgiveness; create more community; build community support for your practice.

### Health

Get informed; relax in the body; read physical signs; exercise; get some R & R (rest and relaxation); watch your diet and nutrition; consider health care services.

As you've done with Inner State, use Tables 1 and then Table 2 for each of the remaining areas of focus. They include:

**Energy**: Practices that allow you to access, use, and transform your energy. These include those focused on yourself (learning about your own energy and its levels, playing with it, purifying, creating intentions, working with a master), and those focused on others (transmitting energy, working with energies of groups and those around you).

**Thoughts**: Practices that address your thoughts and lead you to greater awareness (transforming and mastering thoughts, setting a context, shifting your focus and expectations).

**Emotions and Fears**: Energetic practices for releasing and transforming emotions and fears and not being affected by them (witnessing, dropping self-judgment).

**Self-Expression**: Communication practices and ways to express yourself in new ways, including authentic listening and expression, speaking up, serving, balancing aspects of yourself.

**Relationships**: Building relationships with family, friends, loved ones, and community through new ways of interacting and communicating.

**Health**: Improving your health through a variety of practices, including rest, exercise, diet, and work with health care practitioners.

**Interrelationships between questions (themes) and practices (areas of focus)**

Just by looking at the labels, it's evident that there's a direct relationship between some of the self-inquiry themes and practice areas: Emotions-Emotions, Relationships-Relationships. Then there's Focus and Attention/Perspectives about Life and the World (themes) related to Thoughts (area of focus). Self-Awareness (theme) is related to Inner State (area of focus).

Questions across all themes relate to Inner State practices. In other words, you'll be directed to Inner State practices by many of your answers to questions. Not surprisingly, the questions you ask yourself within Sadhana/Spiritual Practices will lead you to many of the practice areas, especially those related to your Inner State and Energy, Self-Expression and Health. Questions about Emotions will lead you to practices of Self-Expression and Relationships, in addition to the Emotion practices.

**Carrying out this step**

As is clear in the previous section, it may be easy for you to identify the practice area based upon the questions you're asking yourself. For example, you may have some fear and go directly to the Emotions theme for self-inquiry. Then you know without a doubt to go to the Emotions and Fears practice area. Perhaps you're having problems in a relationship with your partner. You ask yourself the Relationships questions, and then go directly to the Relationships practice area.

In choosing your practice area of transformation, think about answers to the questions you've been asking yourself, use Table 2, and skim Appendix 2. The choice should be obvious from what you've learned about yourself and what's included in the practice areas.

**Illustrative Example**

Let's go back to Will Powers. Remember, he realized he's committed and wants to be more powerful in taking action to further his cause.

Through his self-inquiry, if Will realizes he has some fears about taking action related to his cause, he may focus on the Emotions and Fears practice area. If he has some limiting thoughts about himself that stop him from fully expressing himself, he may go to the Thoughts practice area. If he feels he needs to communicate in a new way, be more articulate, and share more of himself, he may go to the Self-Expression practice area.

Will realizes the last alternative fits him the best. He knows he has to be more articulate, expressive, and impactful in how he comes across. Therefore, he chooses Self-Expression as his practice area.

## Step 3: Identifying Specific Practices

You now know which practice area you'll focus on to transform based on what you've learned about yourself through self-inquiry. In this step you'll examine the specific practices within this area of focus so you can identify which to pursue, either without formal planning or with an action plan (Step 4).

Go to Appendix 2 and review all of the practices listed in the area of focus you've chosen. Depending upon what you wish to transform, it should be clear which specific practice(s) you're to choose. Take your time to feel which practice is right for now, because you'll be devoting time to it. The practice is to be the one that's of greatest service to you, and that you know you can commit to thoroughly. In addition to having the strongest relationship with what you wish to transform, and how you'd like to be and act in the world, it should be a practice you're drawn to and one that doesn't feel like work to you. You know it's best for you; it's top priority for your transformation. It's even better if it brings you joy to practice it. Of course, practices for eliminating fears and unwanted emotions may not bring you joy, but you know deep down they're necessary.

When you've decided on the practice, see whether it stands on its own for your transformation right now. If it does, fine. If there's some other practice that will reinforce it or support you to transform even more, then add that one. Don't overload with too many practices. You may decide to stay in the same practice area and choose another practice that complements the one you chose. Or you may decide to choose one option in this practice area and another in a different area.

**Supporting practices.** There are four practices that support you during all of the steps of the transformational journey, meaning you can decide to carry them out when you're reflecting, choosing other practices, and creating and implementing your action plan. We already covered the first one during Step 1. The practices are: *writing* (journaling), *reading* (e.g., books), *listening* (e.g., CDs) and *watching* (e.g., DVDs). These practices transform you by offering information, education, words, sounds, and vibration. They support other practices you carry out. For example, they may provide techniques for meditation, communication and exercise, or a means for you to chant, move, and dance.

Appendix 3 contains a list of suggested books, as well as CDs and DVDs. Use these suggestions to add reading, listening, and/or watching to your practices. They'll inform you before and as you transform, and will contribute to your transformation.

### Illustrative Example

Let's review what runs through Will's head as he goes through Appendix 2 and the specific practices related to Self-Expression.

*"Let's see. Practices for better communication that builds closer relationships: authentic listening, authentic expression? Perhaps this will work. I'll come back to that. Practices related to devotion and doubt? Not really. Speaking up? That sounds good, too. Saying yes more? No, I don't think so. Life changes and creating? No, not right for now. Simplifying, serving? Perhaps later, but not for where I need to transform now. Masculine and feminine sides? No way.*

*"So ... I end up with authentic listening, authentic expression, and speaking up. Well, I think I'm a really good listener. It's more about expressing. This practice of authentic expression asks me to think about an example of where I'm holding back and not expressing myself to someone, and to take action around this. Having an authentic conversation with this person. Well, Joe comes to mind. That would really help. It gets me to be honest and let him know what I think, what my opinion is about this cause. It gets us to work on our relationship so we're able to more powerfully express our commitment together.*

*"When I actually look at the practice of speaking up, that's more about where people haven't spoken up when they disagreed with something or someone. That's not the case with me so I guess I'm going to go with authentic expression. That feels right as my top priority right now."*

We'll come back to this example in the next step.

## Step 4: Creating the Action Plan

Take a look at Diagram 2 on page 15, and let's review the format of the action plan.

**Practice**: In the left-hand column, you place the area of focus of the practice(s) you chose, along with a short summary of the specific activities you'll carry out.

**Time**: This indicates the length of time it will take you to carry out the activity, and whether you're doing it in the morning, afternoon and/or evening. You can also add exact date(s) and time of day. For example, if this is one conversation, you may have a date and time, however you don't have to indicate the length of time if it doesn't serve. If it's an ongoing practice, such as meditation, you can put the time of day you'll be practicing and leave it at that. You decide on what you place here. The criterion is whatever facilitates your transformation.

**Frequency**: This is for activities that you repeat more than once. For example, if you're exercising, going to the health club, you can put the number of times you go per week or per month. If it's a regular activity with no prescribed frequency, you can put "ongoing." If you're meditating, you can put "daily," and the time column gives more specifics about the day.

**With Whom**: This indicates the *major* people involved with you in carrying out the activities you list in the first column. This could be a family or community member, a friend or colleague, a teacher or master. This person is engaged in the activities and provides a contribution to your transformation through this involvement.

**Resources**: These may be additional people, or a group or team, who are involved and not the major players in serving your transformation through the specific activities. They could be people with whom you discuss your transformation or reflect with or practice ahead of time what you're going to do. These could be community members, or someone you partner with to ask each other questions or to practice together. Three other resources are: information or education you require to carry out the activities (e.g., articles, books, CDs, DVDs, classes); finances to fund your activities (specific amount or range); and technology or supplies you may require (e.g., Internet, software, equipment).

**DIAGRAM 2:**
**Transformation Action Plan**

| Practice | Time | Frequency | With Whom | Resources |
|---|---|---|---|---|
| -Area of focus<br>-Specific activity | -Length (how long)<br>-am/pm<br>-Date, time | - Daily<br>-Weekly (times/wk)<br>-Monthly (times/mo)<br>-Ongoing | Major person(s) involved | -Other people<br>-Information/ education<br>-Finances<br>-Technology/ supplies |

## Approach to developing and carrying out the plan

**Relationship to your transformation.** Remember that for the fulfillment of your plan, whether it's a written action plan or just one in your head, you're to be clear about how you relate to your transformation. In other words, how do you see yourself as you transform? Are you committed, focused, disciplined? Are you willing and passionate? Are you doubting or judging yourself? Your relationship with your transformation can change over time. You're to check in regularly to ensure the relationship is facilitating and not hindering your transformation. You may actually need to transform your thoughts or feelings about yourself and your transformation, meaning choose practices in the areas of emotions or thoughts.

**Vision and intention.** Related to your overall transformational journey, you visualize yourself and who you're being given your transformation in many areas of your life. In addition to this general vision of yourself, you create different visions of yourself based on specific areas where you're focusing your transformation. All of these visions inform one another and impact the results of your transformation.

In creating a vision, you come from the heart and not the mind. You breathe and align with higher aspects of yourself, truths that lie deep within your heart. You use your imagination and intuition. You call forth images of yourself and anyone else who's involved, how you look, how you're expressing yourselves. You allow images to come forth, along with any associated feelings and sensations. You don't censor what appears as you focus on your overall transformation or a specific transformation in a certain area of your life.

In our illustrative example, Will Powers has a vision of himself related to where he wishes to transform, his self-expression. He sees himself powerfully articulating the mission of the cause he's committed to. He visualizes himself speaking in front of his coworkers and community members, inspiring them to share a common mission and create a new future together. Everyone is smiling, sitting forward in their seats, saying "yes" as he speaks the vision and the path toward it. He sees himself raising his arms, speaking authentically from his heart, with great power and passion. People in the back of the hall are standing up to see him and cheer him on.

When you clearly see and deeply feel your vision, you have a rich context in which to create your intention. The intention you set is what you'd like to manifest in achieving your vision. It includes specific qualities you and others express, actions you take, and results you achieve. Your intention is the driving force that propels you to achieve your vision. It represents a declaration or a commitment for something to manifest in your world. When you have a vision and intention, you manifest what you envision and intend because of your clarity and focus, the powerful energy you create, and the consistent actions you take.

Let's return to Will. By powerfully and authentically expressing who he is and what he believes, Will intends that everyone agree to take immediate action to make the changes he's recommended. Many volunteers will make agreements for action within specific time frames. Will's intention also includes the qualities of agreement, passion, clarity, commitment, and unity of purpose for himself and everyone involved.

Let's take a different example. Jill Flowers is carrying out practices for building her relationship with her husband Bob. Her vision is both of them walking in nature arm in arm, holding one another, smiling, speaking softly, and feeling completely relaxed and comfortable in each other's company. Her intention is that certain qualities be present in their relationship, including passion, intimacy, appreciation, joy, and playfulness. We come back to Jill later.

You have your vision for yourself. You declare your intention for what's to be present. You hold onto both of these as you carry out your action plan. As you transform, you remind yourself of your vision and intention, no matter what's happening while you're transforming. As you come back to these, you become centered and aligned; you keep on track.

**Flexibility and empowerment of the action plan**. While you're carrying out practices, you can adjust the action plan to make it more powerful and effective. You can add people and resources, or activities such as new conversations or additional steps. Once you're satisfied with the results of your transformation, you debrief within yourself and/or with others. You may choose to create a new plan or revise the original one, going back to the beginning of the transformational journey to self-inquiry. Or you may skip self-inquiry and go directly to the next steps if you know exactly where you want to transform.

The action plan empowers you to transform by clarifying what you're to do and providing parameters for your actions. You're to regard and use the plan as a tool with guidelines, not as a strict rulebook you have to follow to the word. Just the fact that you're setting down these actions and supporting information moves your transformation forward through your clarity, intention, commitment, and agreement with yourself. The plan also gives you the opportunity to empower yourself, to focus, to continue to make decisions and take action, and persevere until you realize your transformation. These are all aspects of self-mastery (decision, focus, realization).

Thus, the action plan is a tool for self-empowerment because it allows you to be conscious of your actions and progress, or your mistakes, inaction and lack of progress. You can then make a decision to accept everything about yourself, be compassionate, and shift out of self-judgment and suffering when things aren't going as you planned. The plan enables you to ask yourself the question, "Am I empowering or disempowering myself and my transformation right now?" and to act accordingly to express your power and further your transformation.

### Illustrative Examples

Diagram 3 presents an Action Plan for two cases. The first one is Will Powers, the example you've seen throughout the four steps. As you know, his practices relate to Self-Expression.

The second case is Jill Flowers. She continues to work on her relationship with Bob. During her self-inquiry, she focused on the themes of Self-Awareness and Sadhana/Spiritual Practices. Through reflection and journaling, she realized that her practice areas of focus are Inner State and Health. The specific practices she chose for the action plan include continuous breathing, meditation, exercise, and nutrition. Diagram 3 presents the plan she created to carry out these practices.

Use these examples to get a better sense of how to approach your own action plan, as well as the interrelationships of the different categories in the plan.

## DIAGRAM 3:
## Transformation Action Plan–With Examples

| Practice | Time | Frequency | With Whom | Resources |
|---|---|---|---|---|
| **Example 1: Will Powers** | | | | |
| **Area of focus:** Self-Expression | | | | |
| **Activities:** | | | | |
| • Authentic expression: Speak honestly with partner about our relationship. Ask for specific changes to improve relationship. Remember to listen. | Tues. 7 pm, 2 hrs; or Thurs. 6 pm, 2 hrs | NA | Joe Bandwagon | Book on effective communication, DVD on motivational speaking |
| • Schedule planning meeting with other potential team members. | | | Joe, Sharon, Bill, Ted | |
| • Follow up with large group presentation and action planning. | | | | |
| **Example 2: Jill Flowers** | | | | |
| **Areas of focus:** Inner State, Health | | | | |
| **Activities:** | | | | |
| • Inner State: continuous breathing | During am/pm meditations | 5 times/week; 2 times/day for 2 mins | Alone | Internet to learn breathing practices |
| • Inner State: meditation | 7 am, 30 mins 9 pm, 15 mins. | 5 times/week | Alone (with Bob?) | Meditation book and/or DVD |
| • Health: aerobic exercise | 7:30 am, 15 mins | 3 times/week | Alone | Buy a treadmill and scale |
| • Health: better nutrition-vegetarian meals | All meals; prepare vegetarian dinners at home | Ongoing | Bob | Vegetarian cookbook, cooking class, nutrition articles |

# SUMMARY

Here's a listing of the highlights of the four steps on your transformational journey:

- You *reflect about yourself and your life*. You choose themes for self-inquiry, questions you'll ask yourself because they're very pertinent to you and where you feel you might need to transform.

- You *ask yourself questions*. You reflect. You journal. You gain awareness of yourself and your life. You get clearer about how to proceed to transform.

- You *identify one or more areas in which to focus your practices* for transformation.

- You *choose specific practices* in the area(s) that are top priority for you to transform.

- You *create an action plan* for carrying out those practices, including specific activities, timing, frequency. You also include major players who'll be involved with the activities, as well as the resources (other people, information, finances, technology).

- You reflect about your *relationship to your transformation*, in order that you be fully committed, focused and disciplined.

- You create and hold a *vision* for who you're being as a result of your transformation, and an *intention* for what will be created in your world when you achieve this vision (the qualities that are present for you and whoever else is involved).

- You *carry out the practices* in the action plan, and/or other practices. You may choose to journal, read, listen and/or watch. You de-brief within yourself, and with others if appropriate.

# CONCLUSION

This workbook provides you with a practical approach and useful information and tools. Through these, you'll be more equipped to transform yourself, your life, and the world you live in. Use this guide however you decide. Know that what's included here serves its purpose only to the extent that you're fully engaged in your own transformation, that you're willing, focused, and disciplined. In other words, *resolve to evolve*.

This guide is one source of support, added to the contributions that others can make in your lives, including your family, friends, communities, teachers, masters. Bring all of these resources together for your own transformation. As you transform, you serve those you know and love, as they serve you.

Make full use of what's being provided here, the tips. Go inside and become aware of what you're to transform, and the actions you're to take to transform. Use your imagination, which is a gift of God. Visualize yourself being the person you wish to be, manifesting what you intend for yourself and your time on this planet. Do the work of transformation, meaning reinvent, recreate yourself rather than making surface changes that don't last. Transform your inner state and outer physicality. Transform the energies you embody and radiate. Transform your thoughts, emotions, words, and actions.

Through this transformation, you'll live a life of vitality and passion. You'll move from fear to love, from suffering to the joy of life, from reaction to creation. You'll be whom you are meant to be, one with Spirit expressed in physical form. In this state of being light you'll serve humanity. Through our collective transformation and service, we'll all live a life we love and bring forth together a new age of divine love in action on the planet.

# APPENDIX 1

## *Individual Questions by Theme*

### SELF-AWARENESS
### SENSE OF SELF/INNER STATE

- "Who am I?" I hear you saying to yourself with disbelief, "What a first question! Is he kidding? This question can last me all my life or longer." Okay, you're right. Still, ask yourself the question, and see what comes. Does the answer show you something about your identity and what you base it on (e.g., your background, title, job)? Does it show you what you value in life, what you are passionate about? Does it highlight your gifts and talents? Does it point out how you want other people to see you? Let your answer inform you about where you focus your attention in relationship to how you view yourself in this life.

- Take a look at how satisfied you are in life. Ask yourself, "Am I fulfilled in my life, or am I longing for something that's missing?" If you feel something's missing, do you know what it is, or is it a vague feeling of longing, emptiness, being incomplete? Stay with this feeling and see where it takes you.

- Devotion. Are you devoted? In what sense? To a person, to a cause, to a guru? If you are, how do you express it, and what does this devotion bring to your life?

- We could say that faith isn't just about religion. It's about our perspectives on life, each other, and ourselves. What is faith for you? Would you say you have faith? What does it feel like? What does it bring into your life? How does it affect your actions? Would you like to develop more faith in yourself and in your life?

- *Surrender,* a word that causes such reaction. We're not talking about cowboys and indians. Just surrender, and answer these questions: "What do I think and feel when I hear the word *surrender*? Do I know how to surrender? Am I surrendering now? What does surrendering look and feel like? Is it an action or a state or both?"

- We're to be in harmony within ourselves and in the world. Have you found inner harmony? Do you feel more natural and at ease in nature? In certain locations? With certain people?

# Approach to living life

- We have many dimensions within ourselves to access and realize. Have you become aware of any higher aspects of yourself? How did you discover them? Are you expressing them in your life?

- There's so much awaiting us in our lives; if we only knew it and opened up. Maybe you do realize this, and more power to you if you do. Would you call yourself adventurous? Do you look for novelty or surprises in your life, or do you resist new things, people, or situations?

- Living life in a state of wonder, open to new beginnings and learning in each moment. Sound good? Ask yourself, "Do I see myself as a beginner in many instances, open to learning and seeing situations afresh? Do I see and seek opportunities in life for gaining new knowledge and learning new things? Do I have a sense of wonder about what's to come and the sense that it's just the beginning of much more?"

- We can be willing or resigned in life, open or closed to taking action, especially during major transitions. Here are some questions about your willingness to go for it and act: "Do I approach life saying yes or no most of the time? Would I say I'm ready and willing no matter what? What's my view about free will and the power of will?"

- Many of us complicate our lives with our thoughts, our plans, our busyness. Think about these: "How can I simplify my life? How can I simplify my thoughts? What effects will this simplicity have on different areas of my life?"

# Commitment

- Commitment represents a decision that leads to action with focus and dedication. We may express this commitment in different ways. Reflect about your own commitment: "What am I most committed to in my life? Are these commitments clear to me? How do I express them? Do I remind myself of these commitments over time? How can I be more committed?"

- When we commit, we're taking a stand for what we believe in, what we know to be true or important in our lives. Ask yourself about your commitment: "Do I have strong commitments in life? Do I express them confidently, powerfully, passionately? Or do I have difficulty expressing or following through on some or all of them?"

# Personal changes and evolution

- Life is continuous learning, a series of new insights and awakenings. What have you learned about yourself recently? Are you applying what you learned in your life at home, at work, in your relationships? In developing your knowledge or capabilities? What else can you do to apply what you've learned?

- At some point, we all come to a crossroads in our lives where we're required to take stock and contemplate where we are and where we want to go. Are you at that point? Ask yourself, "Where am I going? Do I feel a need to go in a new direction? If yes, in what area(s) of my life? What does this new direction look like, feel like?"

- We don't usually count the transitions in our lives, however there are many. Are you going through any transitions in your life right now? What makes this a transition? What does it look like and feel like? Will any changes on your part make this transition smoother?

- Ask yourself about what grades you're getting in your life: "Can I identify events that happened in my life that I would call 'tests'? Did I pass them or fail? What do I call failing? What do I call passing? Did I attract them into my life? For what reason?"

- When we're in a spiritual path, we focus on our personal transformation. We carry out certain practices that enable us to go within, realize ourselves, and live life as Spirit. Would you say you're in a spiritual path? If yes, what makes you say this? Ask yourself whether you're "in" it or "on" it, where the former means you're focused, disciplined, and committed. If you're "on" it and not "in" it, what can you do to be more "in" it?

# Energy

- Masters have repeated the same teachings for centuries. So why not join the group and repeat the following: *We're all energy. Everything is energy.* Now ask yourself, "How aware am I of my own energy and how I'm using it in my practice and daily life? How much have I studied energy and its use? How much more would I like to learn about different energies and how to use them in my life? Do I know people or have resources I can find to learn about energy?"

# Perspectives About Life and the World
## View of what life offers

- Being open or closed in how we view different situations and life in general determines how we act, how effective we are, and how fulfilled we can be. Related to this, answer these two questions: "Do I more easily see possibilities or limitations in my life? Would

I call myself optimistic or pessimistic, creative or reactive?" Think about it, and be honest with yourself.

- Maa is the embodiment of Mahalakshmi, the goddess of abundance and prosperity. What's your perspective on abundance? Abundance of what? Do you trust in the universe and its abundance? Do you agree that everything's waiting for you to tap into and realize it?

- In many circles, miracles have a religious connotation, or they're thought of as very rare or extraordinary events. Have there been any miracles in your life? Are there any now? Are you open to them happening in your life?

- With regard to the perfection of the divine unfoldment: is there someone out there or in here orchestrating this? Answer these questions: "Have people, places, or situations from the past shown up in my life again later on? What are some examples? How did I react? Do I feel there's a reason for this? If yes, what is it? Do I believe in coincidences, in synchronicity? What about fate and destiny?"

## SENSE OF TIME AND LIFE EXPERIENCE

- Many have lived on this planet before us. Are they still here? Are they serving us or having some influence on us in this life? Think about those individuals who are closely linked to you and your family: "Do I ever feel connected to those who have come before me—my ancestors, past generations? Have I studied my family tree? Am I connected to any spiritual lineage from a certain faith or tradition? Does any of this interest me, and do I want to learn more?"

- "I could swear I know that person." "I feel very close to her and I don't know why." "This place is familiar. I'm sure I've been here before." Have you felt this with any people or in different places in your life? Has this been happening more frequently in your life? If yes, how do you explain this?

- "Is this all there is?" Have you asked yourself this question? Ask yourself now, "Is this the only life I have? Are there more life experiences in store for me? Have I lived past lives? What do I think about reincarnation?"

- Maybe you couldn't express it as much before, but now you can. Have there been repeated circumstances in your life that have given you the opportunity to express yourself, your skills, and what you've learned in new or more powerful ways? Are there any opportunities now for you?

- "Time stands still." "Time waits for no man (or woman)." "I'll think about that tomorrow." "It seems like yesterday." Here are some time questions for you: "What's my perspective on time? Is it linear? How do I see the relationship between the past, present, and future? Are they distinct, or are we living them all at the same time? Does my view of time include past lives? Do I think experiences in this life are related to past life experiences?"

## SPIRITUALITY

- Religion is about man-made belief systems, and spirituality is universal and about the Spirit. What's your view on religion and spirituality? Are they the same? Does your view of one influence the other?

- Maybe you've heard about other masters, or met some, or have one in your life. What's your perspective about spiritual teachers, enlightened masters, and gurus? Do you have one in your life? Are you interested in taking any steps to find out more?

- If you have an enlightened master or guru in your life, what do you see as the benefits? How would you describe your devotion and commitment to the master or guru? How do you describe it to others, or don't you?

- What's your take on enlightenment, being in the light? Do you have your own definition? Have you discussed enlightenment with others, or studied it, read about it? What's your attitude about it, your relationship with it? Do you hold it as a goal or objective in your life?

- What about ascension? Have you ever heard about it, thought about it? Do you think ascension, perhaps along with enlightenment, are absurd concepts having nothing to do with you? Or are you engaged with them and how they play out in your life?

## FOCUS AND ATTENTION
## INTERNAL/EXTERNAL

- Many of us have heard about intrinsic and extrinsic motivation. Even if you haven't, ask yourself these questions. Become more conscious of where you focus, and let your answers speak to you about whether you'd like to make any change in your focus: "Am I driven by outside goals, outcomes, and results, such as recognition, money, or advancement? Am I motivated internally by living my life in a certain way, according to certain values? What are the consequences? How do I feel? Am I contented? What is the quality of my relationships and interactions in the world?"

- Our inner lives are rich with great wisdom and power. The spiritual path is about focusing on and benefiting from what our inner lives have to offer. Ask yourself, "Do I focus more within myself or outside? When I focus outside, what am I focusing on? Do I use any practices for inner work, contemplation, or meditation? If not, would I like to?"

# HEART/MIND

- We tend to be focused either in the mind or the heart. From what I've experienced, a higher percentage focuses in the mind, including me for many years. We can develop a close relationship between the two. What do you think or feel, or both, about any or all of these questions: "Am I more of a thinker or feeler? Do I spend most of my time in my mind or my heart? Am I guided more by one than the other? What touches me the most in my heart or impacts me the most in my mind? Can I achieve more balance between the two?"

- How do we know what's best for us? Our parents may not be around anymore. Do we have a little voice whispering in our ear? I'd love to know who that is. Answer this: "Do I always know what's best for me? Can I access this easily within myself in different situations? Do I get the answer in my mind, my heart, my gut?"

# BROAD/NARROW AND TIME FOCUS

- Thinking about the whole picture, the context, ask yourself, "Do I see the whole picture when something happens, or do I focus on one part? Do I identify trends, patterns, and transitions in my life? If yes, do I give them a meaning that serves me to understand them, myself, or my life better?"

- Spend some time on these time questions: "Where do I focus most of my attention—on the present, past, or future? When I stay in the present moment, what do I experience or feel like? How willing am I to start living in the present more? Am I committed to stay in the present, to come back to it when I start thinking about what may happen in the future or when I go back to what happened in the past?"

- "Should I plan it out or just let it happen?" Do you ask yourself this question? What about these questions: "What role does planning play in my life? Do I see myself as 'planful' and structured, or spontaneous and intuitive in my approach to life? What are the consequences for me of my approach?"

- Don't analyze, just reflect: "Do I analyze and process before making decisions and taking action? If yes, does this analysis and processing usually serve me? Will it serve me to practice being more spontaneous and in the flow?"

# DISTRACTIONS AND EGO

- Sometimes we grow up "attached to our mother's apron strings." What are you attached to in your life? To which people? To what possessions? To what aspects of yourself? What does this attachment feel like? What are the consequences for your self-expression?

- We're bombarded with distractions in our lives, meaning distractions from going within, learning about ourselves, and transforming: TV, cell phones, websites, iPods, iPads, and so on. Of course, these have benefits. We need to ask ourselves how we use them in our lives and whether they take over. Here are some questions you may want to ask yourself: "Am I distracted from taking a closer look at myself? Am I creating distractions in my life? Are my thoughts and actions focused on satisfying my senses and desires and certain addictions? Am I satisfied with this? What are the consequences for my health and well being?"

- We can be on a steady course, knowing where we're going and what we're doing. Or we can doubt—doubt ourselves or doubt where we'll end up. Ask yourself, "Do I tend to doubt more than trust? Do I doubt myself? Do I doubt others? What are the consequences of my doubt?"

- We can intensify or prolong suffering in our lives when we place too much meaning on situations and weigh them down with significance. Ask yourself, "Is there anything I hold as very significant and meaningful in my life that troubles me and causes me to suffer? Do I create stories around this? How can I shift my thinking to make it less significant and have less influence on me and my life?"

- The law of attention. What we place our attention on, we bring into our life. Some say we are what we place our attention on. Reflect on this: "Am I placing attention right now on something that's causing me discomfort, or have I done this in the past? Do I tend to magnify what's not working, what's not feeling comfortable, through my attention or thoughts? How can I shift my focus to feel better, to be more content?"

- We don't really share our fantasies with others, do we? They're for us. What do we do with them? How much time do we spend with them? Here are some questions for you to ask yourself if you dare: "How much do I fantasize? What do I fantasize about? Are there common themes? What do these themes show me about myself? Do I focus more on my fantasies than my actual love life? Do I fantasize before relationships, or during relationships? Do my fantasies supply me with something that I feel is missing in my life and relationship(s)? Can I control my fantasy life, or do my fantasies control me?"

## FEMININE/MASCULINE

- We've grown up with so many messages about the characteristics and importance of what's masculine and what's feminine. We have prejudices that are being revealed and are up for transformation in many of us now. Take a look at your perspective, and see what you want to do about it: "Which would I say is stronger in me, my masculine or feminine side? Or are they balanced? How do I define each? What does each feel like? What behaviors are associated with each? What's my perspective on the divine feminine and its value, its role in my life, and its effect on the planet?"

- "What do I think about the union of the feminine and masculine within me (*Shiv-Shakti*)? Do I understand this? Do I see this as valuable and beneficial?"

# EMOTIONS
# FEARS

- Fears stop us in our tracks. Are you afraid to act or make changes? Reflect and see whether you've hesitated or not acted because you've been afraid. See if you can identify the nature of the fear in one or two major instances. Dig down to see what underlies the fear at the most fundamental level.

- Let's take a look at your fears. Ponder: "What are some things I'm really afraid of in life right now? What's underneath that fear? What's underneath that?" Keep on going until you get to the core of the fear.

- How you see yourself when you're afraid can intensify your fear or diminish it. Move into some fear that you have, and answer these two questions about self-judgment: "Do I judge myself for my fear? If so, does my self-judgment intensify my fear even more?"

# WORRYING

- Some people are professional worriers. See how you answer these questions. Don't worry about your answers: "Am I a worrier? What have been the consequences of my worrying? Do I focus on the future and worry about getting there? Do I carry something from my past that causes me to worry?"

- Think back. Were actual situations as bad as you thought they'd be? Did people react as you thought they would when you worried ahead of time?

# MASTERING MOODS AND EMOTIONS

- We all have buttons that get pushed and triggers that get pulled. "Do my buttons get pushed often or once in a while? What triggers my negative emotions or behaviors? Are there similarities between the people or situations that push my buttons? If yes, what are they and what can they teach me about myself?"

- Our emotions either master us, or we master them. That's doesn't mean we control them. Mastery is about releasing or transforming emotions. Mastery is about being with our emotions in a way that we don't focus on them and they don't bother or impact us. Are there certain emotions you can't master? Is there one prevalent one that keeps on coming up? What consequences are there for your relationships and your being more effective or fulfilled in life?

- We're to get to a state where we're witnessing our thoughts and emotions. How would you rate yourself in witnessing your thoughts and emotions instead of identifying with them or getting enmeshed in them? Are there any deep wounds you're aware of that you'd like to release and transform? Have you spent any time working with these?

- Life transitions. How do you feel when some big change happens in your life? Can you easily shift? Do you become unstable? Do you shut down or open up? Do you react or act?

## Judgment/control/ego

- We're our worst critics. How do you react when you make mistakes? Do you judge yourself? Do you take responsibility for learning or rectifying the situation without self-judgment? What can you change within yourself related to making mistakes?

- Control. We're not talking about air traffic. Being honest with yourself, are you a person who has to know the answer, be right? Do you like to control? Do you control certain people and/or situations in your life? What does this feel like? What do you gain in controlling? What do you lose?

- Do you have many "shoulds" in your life? Do you try and try, and then try again? What about wanting and not having? What can you do to reduce any of these in your mind, in your life?

- The ego is always with us. It's about how we are with the ego. It's about how we are in our lives in relationship to the ego. Do you feel you're separate from everyone else, not connected? What's your feeling about the idea of separation and the ego? Have you experienced the traps and pitfalls of the ego: doubt, judgment, blame, projection, distraction, justification, and arrogance? Which traps are most present in you now? Have any increased lately and, if yes, in what way? What have you done about them?

## Physical impact

- Think about any recurring aches or pains or physical illnesses you've had or have right now. Is your body trying to tell you something about any deep wounds or strong feelings you have within you to confront, accept, and release?

# RELATIONSHIPS
## LOVE/COMPASSION/COMMUNICATION

- Love, loving, being loved. What's your take on love? "Has my definition or understanding of love changed over the years? What does love feel like to me? Do I feel love often in my life? Am I missing that feeling? Am I expressing love often in my life?"

- One way to look at compassion is that it's love with understanding. Ask yourself, "What is compassion for me? Am I compassionate? How can I be more compassionate? Does it matter to me?"

- Take a look at how you communicate. This means listening and expressing. "How authentic am I in sharing with others and expressing what's true for me? Am I vulnerable in my communication and relationships? Do I truly listen to others? Am I present and open to them, or do my stories and judgments about them or what they're saying influence how well I'm listening?"

## CLOSE RELATIONSHIPS (INCLUDING PARTNER, CHILDREN, OTHER FAMILY, FRIENDS)

- Expressing the fullness of who you are. "Am I expressing all of myself with this person (insert my partner, my child, etc.), or keeping parts of myself hidden, unexpressed? Do I play, laugh, cry, and express myself in diverse ways? Am I willing to express more of myself? Which aspects? If not, what is holding me back?"

- Ask yourself about your deep down appreciation of this person and how you express it: "How often do I tell this person I appreciate her, how grateful I am for her presence in my life? Do I point out qualities I love about this person, how she distinguishes herself in life? Do I recognize this person for her accomplishments, abilities, and progress?"

- Ask yourself about doing or being: "Do I focus on entertaining this person, keeping busy, giving gifts, and satisfying desires? Or do I focus on the quality of our time together, how we're being with one another, the love, joy, playfulness, and laughter we experience together? Do I schedule all my time with this person, or am I spontaneous and just see what happens?"

- Joy has no reason. "Am I joyful? How do I express joy with this person? Are there aspects of joy that are missing in my life? How can I rejoice more with this person? Do we dance together, literally and figuratively? Do we have fun together? Are we both free in each other's presence?"

- Take a look at your moods when you're with this person: "Do I let it go on for a long period of time when I get into a mood, when I fight or argue, when I don't speak? Do

I close up, withdraw, and remove myself from the situation? Or do I act quickly and transform what's happened, shifting my mood, feelings, and behaviors right away?"

- Ask yourself about expectations and imposing your opinion: "Are there things I would love to see this person doing that he isn't doing? Am I disappointed? Do I impose my opinion on this person about what I like, my preferences for his interests, pursuits, and actions? Do I let this person be and just provide guidance when asked?"

- Caring and serving: "How do I care for and serve this person? Do I care or serve at all? What does caring and serving look like? What else can I do, how different can I be, to express this caring and service more in our relationship?"

- In many relationships, we expect and carry baggage. What about you? "Do I hold expectations of my partner that come from my past, my parents' relationship, and/ or previous relationships I've had? Do I see my partner for who he is? Do I hold my partner up against certain standards that are hard to meet? How can I change or drop my expectations?"

- Ask yourself about the tug of war with your children—using your children as substitutes. "Do I put my child in the middle? Between my partner and me? Between me and anyone with whom I'm fighting or not getting along? Do I rely on my child to supply me with what's missing in the relationship with my partner or with anyone in my life? Do I take care of my child, or does my child take care of me? Do I look for something in my child that's inappropriate or impossible, to be found instead in my relationship with someone else or within myself?"

## COMMUNITY/DIVERSITY

- Creating community supports your transformation in the path and the evolution of the planet. "Where two or more are gathered in my name, there will I [God] be also." Reflect about your relationship to community: "Am I creating community in my life? What communities am I part of? Am I being supported and supporting others in the community? Is there any community I can join or create that will serve me and everyone?"

- Our families and communities can be so powerful in our lives. Do you receive support in your spiritual path for your practices and way of life? From your family? At work? In your community? Are you a member of any spiritual community or group in which you meditate, discuss spiritual life, and practice together? Do you feel alone or part of community in the path?

- You've heard about "unity in diversity." Answer these questions about diversity: "Do I value diversity in my life? How diverse are my relationships? Do I expose myself to diverse people and situations? How can I increase diversity in my life right now?"

# LEADERSHIP

- There are so many perspectives on leadership. Let's take one—Empowerment. Ask yourself: "What is empowerment? Would I call myself an empowering leader? Do I empower myself? In what ways? Do I empower others to express themselves and their leadership? What can I do to transform my leadership to be more empowering?"

# SADHANA/SPIRITUAL PRACTICES

- We speak about daily practices, being devoted, focused, and disciplined. They're spiritual practices in the sense that as you transform through them, you live more spiritually. Do you have a spiritual practice or *sadhana*? Would you say you're devoted to it? In what ways does this devotion show up? Are you disciplined? Do you regularly take time for your practice and stick to what you've decided to do?

- What specific practices, if any, do you have (e.g., breathing, meditation, *japa* or repeating mantras, being in nature, exercising, yoga, diet, chanting, movement)? Do you focus on some more than others? Do you jump around? Do you have a sense of which serve you the most?

- We benefit from practice. What do you feel are the benefits of your *sadhana*? What are your favorite practices? Why? Are there any changes you would make to your *sadhana* now so that it's more beneficial?

- Yes, spiritual practice is "doing the work," the work of transformation. At the same time, it doesn't have to be work or effort. Does your spiritual practice bring you joy, or do you experience it as work, effort, something you have to do? How can you instill more joy in your *sadhana*?

- You may have heard, "You're not the doer," or "It's not about doing, it's about being." Take a look at your focus: "Do I balance doing and being? Do I schedule all my time to accomplish and achieve, or do I also schedule time to rest, to be still, to be by and within myself? Do I keep on doing to avoid seeing something in myself?"

- Do you forget to breathe? Are you breathing right now? More questions: "Do I use different breathing techniques? Which ones? What are the effects of each?"

- One of the most important parts of our spiritual practice is meditation. What kind(s) of meditation do you practice? Stillness? Guided? What differences do you find within yourself based upon the type of meditation you practice?

- With regard to reciting sacred sounds and benefiting from the power of sound and vibration, do you recite mantras? What are your favorite mantras? Why? What are the effects?

- We can express ourselves on so many levels. What do you feel about chanting? About movement and dance? Do you resist or feel self-conscious, or are you free when you chant or dance?

- We need to take care of the vehicle through which we live and express ourselves as Spirit. Do you exercise enough according to what's needed for the health and well-being of your body? Would you like to add any more forms of exercise to your life? Stretching, aerobic, and/or strength training?

- Remember, we are what we eat. Do you pay attention to your diet, to nutrition? Are you a vegetarian? If yes, do you notice a difference from when you weren't? What are your favorite foods? Are they "good" for you? Do you care?

- R & R (& R). Rest and relaxation (and release). Do you find time to rest and relax? Can you find more? How much do you smile? How much do you laugh? Can you bring more smiles and laughter into your life through certain people or situations that make you laugh or just by smiling and laughing more? Do you let it all out by screaming, crying, and/or moving the body?

- The joy of serving. Have you experienced this? Have you engaged in any *seva*, or selfless service, in your life? Do you understand what it means to be selfless in your actions? Is service important to you? If you've done *seva*, has your experience of *seva* or your perspective about it changed over time? Has this impacted the *seva* you choose to do or how you approach it?

# APPENDIX 2

## *Individual Practices by Area of* ⌐ ⌐

### INNER STATE

(Creating or shifting your state)

- **Breathe!** Devoting time to breathe naturally is so rare yet so important. Take a moment now. Take time every day to be aware of your breath. Open and relax, and allow each inhale and exhale to come naturally.

  Try different breathing practices. There's the cyclical or continuous breath, where you breathe through the nose (always the best way to get oxygen in your lungs), and don't pause between the inhale and the exhale. This breath moves you into the zone, a state of deep peace. Try the *oujai* breath by breathing through your nose and making a sound in your throat like you do when you're sleeping deeply, like the sound of an ocean wave. The back of your throat is closed. Another practice is breathing through the nose slowly, eyes closed and focusing your attention between your two eyebrows. This is a point of stillness that brings you to deep inner silence.

- **Slow down with the breath**. If you're having many thoughts, an overly active mind that doesn't allow you to rest or be peaceful, then breathe. Accept everything that's happening within you. See whether you can move into a state with a natural, conscious breath where you witness the thoughts without holding onto them, without evaluating them or trying to stop them. You may choose to breathe cyclically or continuously. You may choose to focus on the heart and to feel love, which can increase the stillness and relaxation. You may choose to breathe into different parts of the physical body from the head gradually moving to the feet, concentrating on creating a relaxed and expanded state in each part.

- **Reallocate your time to go within**. Take a few moments to review your daily and weekly schedule. Determine what time you can free up to be still in order to sit and breathe consciously. See whether you're spending an inordinate amount of time focusing on the outside world, pursuing your desires, and satisfying your senses.

ermine how you will schedule more of your time to be quiet and sit in stillness
in order to achieve more balance in your life. Take time on a regular basis to reflect
about yourself and your life. Ask yourself questions. Keep a journal. Walk in nature,
focusing on your breath and inner state. Go inside when you wake up and when you
go to rest the body, even if only for a few minutes. It doesn't have to take hours to
spend time with yourself.

- **Practice "Nowism."** With conscious breath, practice being in the moment, breathing,
  walking consciously, eating consciously in silence, showering, and doing whatever
  you're doing with awareness. Witness whether you're doing or being. Practice being
  aware of your thoughts and feelings in the moment. Notice whether you're in the past
  or future, and come back to the present. Experiment with creating positive thoughts
  and feelings in the moment. Make this a regular practice, at least several times a
  week, in different settings and circumstances. Notice the effect it has on you, your
  consciousness, your state of being, and your actions.

- **Meditate.** Research different possibilities for learning how to meditate if you don't
  already know. Find books and/or teachers. Visit the Humanity In Unity website for
  any programs about meditation and other daily practices (www.HumanityInUnity.
  org). Learn about Stillness Meditation, which takes us from gross thought deep into
  our true Self (www.sai-maa.com). Meditation doesn't have to last three hours a day,
  sitting in lotus position with complicated *mudras* (finger positions). If you have been
  meditating for a while, experiment with other types of meditation if you feel this
  serves you.

Here's a simple meditation, "Coming Home" (two more meditations are provided at
the end of this section):

*Sitting comfortably, close your eyes and breathe consciously. Notice and appreciate
each breath. Allow each breath to bring with it more and more peace and stillness. Now
breathe into your heart and rest there, expanding in the love that resides there. Love your
breath; love this moment. Expand even more in this love. With your breath, allow this
love to move throughout your entire physical form, from just above your head to just
below your feet. Allow the movement of this vibration of love to flow freely for several
minutes throughout the physical form.*

*Now breathe just above your head, and move with the breath farther above the head
with all the love in your heart. Embrace your expansion into the higher realms above
you. Call upon these realms, what you may call the Presence, the Self, or the Source.
Merge with this high vibration of love and light. Breathe deeply and rest in this union,
this homecoming.*

*After several minutes, breathe deeply again and bring this one love, one light, down
into your physical form and deep into the core of your heart. Breathe there, and rest
in the embrace of this love for several minutes. Then, with your breath, become aware*

*of your surroundings, of your physical body, and slowly and gracefully open your eyes. Appreciate and be present with your current state of being.*

- **Create a sacred space.** Going within ourselves to become more aware of who we are takes practice and dedicated time. This doesn't mean you have to meditate for five hours a day. Create a space at home where you sit for even five minutes in stillness, not trying or doing—just being. Create an altar or a surface where you place a few items you love that take you into a restful, peaceful state. These can be photos, crystals, statues, candles, and/or incense. Use the same pillow, perhaps with an *asan*, or covering, or the same shawl; these will serve as reminders for you to take time for yourself when you see them. They also retain your energy from meditation.

- **Use the centering technique.** There's a simple, ancient practice for centering ourselves, a practice that's especially needed in today's world of planetary changes to ensure we're centered and stable. Place one hand next to your navel, opened with fingers pointing up and palm facing sideways toward the body. Raise your other arm straight up with your hand open and palm facing sideways toward the body. Breathe consciously, inhaling in this position, and then exhaling as you lower the one arm slowly and raise the other hand slowly until both hands meet at your heart, palms facing each other in prayer position. Inhale slowly with your hands joined at the heart. With each breath, experience yourself completely centered and aligned throughout the body. Repeat this at least two more times, alternating the position of your two arms.

- **Be grateful.** We speak of gratitude as an attitude of grace, a practice and state that align us with the constant grace that flows from our heart, from our Self. Go to bed and wake up with appreciation and gratitude for yourself, your qualities, and your accomplishments. Be grateful for your partner, children, parents, loved ones, and their presence in your life. Picture them and love them with all your heart. Be grateful for all your relationships. Be grateful for your breath, that you're alive in a physical form that light beings are lined up for centuries to embody.

  Move on to an advanced course in gratitude. Take one week to be grateful for everything in your life, whether the person or situation satisfies you, brings you joy, or whether the person or situation aggravates you or triggers strong emotions. Be grateful for the opportunities to be more aware of yourself, to learn and grow, to express yourself, to accept and transform whatever no longer serves you. Keep coming back to this gratitude no matter how the body is feeling, what the mind is creating, whatever emotions are surfacing and being expressed.

- **Develop love for yourself.** Make a mental and preferably written list of the qualities you like about yourself, your gifts and talents, the multiple dimensions within you. Choose one or two qualities to start out with. Be grateful for them when you go to bed and wake up. See how you can express these qualities even more in your daily life. Experiment. Play. Then choose some other qualities or skills and do the same. When you're appreciating yourself during the day or night, touch your two hands to your heart and breathe in what you love about yourself. Love your breath. Love this moment. Take time to truly rest in this love and appreciation within you.

- **Laugh and be joy-full.** Just take some time each day to laugh, perhaps in the shower. Tell jokes and express your sense of humor in conversations with others. Practice smiling while looking in the mirror when you're brushing your teeth or combing your hair (or shaving your head). Smile when you're with your family, when you're at work, and while you're doing whatever you're doing during the day. Identify what brings you joy in life. Surround yourself with these people, things, places, and situations. Have conversations with others about joy, what it is, and what brings them joy. See what actions you can take together to create more joy in your lives.

- **Practice affirmations with "I am."** Whatever you follow the phrase "I am" with, you manifest in yourself and the world. Use this practice at any time, with focus and intention as you go within, no matter what's happening around you in your daily life. Use it especially during what you might call challenging situations. You can also use this during your meditation practice.

  Close your eyes, move into your heart, and feel what you're reciting. Say the affirmation as many times as you choose until you feel complete. Some affirmations that you can repeat to yourself or aloud include, "I am light," "I am violet light," "I am pure space," "I am peace in manifestation in action," "I am the power of love in action," "I am full self-expression at all times," "I am the grace and beauty of Maa," "I am the realization of Self in manifestation."

- **Recite mantras.** Doing *japa*, or reciting sacred mantras on a 108-beaded necklace or mala, is a common practice for going within, being still, and transforming our state. These mantras or sacred syllables are sounds, said silently or aloud, that evoke the name of God and the energies of divine beings. They're infused with living power, *prana* or life force, that serve to purify us, expand our consciousness, and bring us into a state where we merge with Self. When we repeat them with total devotion, we activate the energy of the deity serving us in our transformation. Mantras have the ability to purify the mind by transforming negative thought forms, dissolving deep patterns and impurities.

  Here are some powerful mantras for you to choose from depending upon what energy you would like to activate within yourself, what attributes you'd like to manifest in your life. Please don't jump around from mantra to mantra; continue with one to notice the effects and benefit from the activation of the energy.

  ➤ Say *Om Gam Gloum Namaha* for Ganesh/Ganapathi to remove obstacles and clear a pathway for you to progress in the path.

  ➤ Say *Om Namah Shivaya* to honor Shiva and to create energy of cleansing and purification, a state of pure space, Shiv.

➤ Say *Guru Om* to activate the love and power of the guru within you ("The guru is in me; I am the guru").

➤ Say *Om Mani Padme Hum* to activate the Buddha of Compassion within.

➤ Say *So Ham*, which means "I am that." When we are born, we inhale *So*, and when we leave the body we exhale *Ham*. This is a natural part of our breath, what we breathe in every moment, every day, a universal vibration. You can use a *mala* for this or not. Close your eyes. Breathe, and say *So* to yourself with the inhalation and *Ham* with the exhalation. Repeat this to yourself for several minutes and appreciate your state of being.

These are the four devi mantras to activate different aspects of the Mother:

➤ *Om Aim Saraswatyai Namaha* (Saraswati, the goddess of knowledge, music, the arts, and speech)

➤ *Om Shrim Mahalakshmyai Namaha* (Lakshmi, the goddess of beauty, grace, abundance, and prosperity)

➤ *Om Dum Mahadurgayai Namaha* (Durga, the goddess of invincibility, who redeems us in situations of utmost distress, riding on a lion and carrying weapons and a lotus flower)

➤ *Om Klim Kalikayai Namaha* (Kali, called the Dark Mother, the fierce goddess who destroys the ego and what no longer serves us).

• **Use the Sri Chakra to unite the divine feminine and masculine.** You can practice the union of *Shiv-Shakti*, the honoring and activation of the Divine Mother within you. The Sri Chakra consists of nine interlocking triangles that surround and radiate out from a central point (*bindu*), representing the relationship between the physical and the unmanifest. The Sri Chakra represents the Goddess in the form of Sri Lalitha or Tripura Sundari. Four of the triangles point up, representing Shiva, and five point downward, representing *Shakti*. This is *Shiv-Shakti*, the union of the divine masculine and feminine.

You can research about the Sri Chakra (e.g., Google, Amazon). Find actual metal or crystal Sri Chakras for your altar if you have one. Say mantras or meditate in front of it, even doing *pujas* (honoring ceremonies) if you choose.

• **Develop the relationship between the mind and the heart.** Maa teaches about loving with the mind and thinking with the heart. There's a strong relationship between the mind and the heart that we can reinforce and embrace within ourselves. Realizing and strengthening this union brings us greater harmony, stability, and power in living our lives. Try this meditation, "Heart and Mind as One":

*With your eyes closed, relax the body with the breath. Breathe deeply into your heart. With each breath, feel the expansion in your heart. Now feel Maa's love, the love of the*

*Divine Mother, within your heart. Breathe, and be touched by the love, tenderness, and compassion expanding and radiating from your heart.*

*Visualize a sphere of golden light penetrating and surrounding your heart. With your breath, intensify this golden light. Move the light throughout your chest, up into your neck and head, and into your brain. Allow this love, this golden light of Mother, to penetrate the brain and spread throughout it. Breathe deeply once again. Realize with your breath the love and power of this sphere of golden light encompassing both your brain and heart. Breathe this loving relationship between your mind and heart. Rest there for several minutes.*

*Now radiate this love of mind and heart, this golden light, throughout your physical form from the top of your head to the bottom of your feet. Spread this oneness of heart and mind deep into all the cells of the body. Breathe and anchor this love throughout your entire being. Appreciate this state for several minutes.*

*Take a deep breath. Become aware of your physical body and surroundings. Slowly open your eyes. What do you feel? Do you feel the mind-heart relationship? Do you feel the love, alignment, harmony, unity, and power that come from this relationship? Using your breath, continue in this same state for the remainder of your day until you go to rest the body.*

- **Radiate coherence.** Coherence is an ongoing practice in life. Maa has spoken of coherence, our being coherent with the energy of the Self, the Presence, and the Source. I wrote an article about this ("Coherence and Creation: A Transformational Model") that you can access on the HIU website. Coherence is like the "clicking in" of a seat belt where the two parts are aligned, fit together, and function as a whole. It's being in agreement, an accord, a "yes" in thoughts, feelings, actions, and energy.

  As a practice, use the following meditation. Notice the different effects it has on you.

  *Breathe naturally, and move into deep stillness within. With your breath, focus and breathe in the heart. Using your intention, the power of mind, and your imagination, align consciously with the highest of who you are: your Self, the Presence, love, truth, and the Source. Realize this alignment as coherence, a coming together, a communion. Create a loving inner dialogue in your heart that increases and sustains this alignment.*

  *Allow yourself to be a movement of coherent waves of energy, a transmission of information signals that flows from your heart throughout your entire physical body. Direct these waves of energy to penetrate the mind located in the brain. Expand it there, and move it up to the higher realms above the head. Express your love, and be grateful for this expansion of energy, this transformation of your state of being. Breathe this gratitude for several minutes.*

  *Realize that you can create from this state. You are a creator who is one with the Source, empowered now and always to invent and manifest in accordance with creation.*

*Visualize any family members, friends, colleagues, or community members. Say within yourself what you wish to say to them from the love in your heart, the purity of your mind, this coherent state of being one with the Source. Be with them for a few moments with this love and expanded energy.*

*Continue and devote your entire being to all of society, to the entire planet. You are a coherent creator aligned with the Self and creation. Create with this inner power. Be a global citizen. Radiate and serve all of humanity as the love and light of the Source. Take a deep breath and expand this contribution even more.*

*Appreciate this moment and be grateful for your incarnation at this important time of transformation on the planet. You are fulfilling your purpose by contributing to a new humanity, a healthy and vibrant planet. Now become aware of your surroundings and body, and slowly open your eyes.*

# ENERGY

(Accessing, using and transforming energy)

## WITHIN YOURSELF:

- **Use your energy.** As Maa teaches, as have other great masters, we're all energy; everything is energy. We're made out of light, sound, and vibration. Once we become more aware of ourselves as energy, of others in our lives and all that's around us as energy, we can access it and use it to transform ourselves, and to serve others and the planet.

  Use the following questions as part of your regular practice. They will assist you in getting a better sense of your own energy, how aware you are of it, and how you're using it or not in your life. Let your answers inform and enrich your practice.

  ➢ How am I to be aware of energy?

  ➢ How am I to understand and best use my energetic potential?

  ➢ How am I to use energy in the proper manner?

  ➢ How am I to be mindful of how I'm using energy in any given moment?

  ➢ How am I to be dynamic and maximize the use of energy?

  ➢ How am I to use my energy to create an impact in my life?

  ➢ How am I to be alert to the use of energy in even the most challenging circumstances?

- **Relate to your own energy.** With your eyes closed, practice being present using your breath. Let your thoughts go by and stay in the moment. Notice what's happening within you with each breath. What's your breath like? What does your body feel like from head to toe? Are there any places that are tight or contracted? Breathe into them and relax. If you choose, slowly open your eyes, notice your energy and state, and then close them again.

With your eyes closed, breathe into your heart. Appreciate each inhalation and exhalation. Be grateful you're alive and breathing. Remember that you're energy, that everything's energy. You have great power within you. After a few minutes, raise your arms very slowly above your head with your palms up, until your arms are straight above your head like a chalice. Breathe and open to the energy, vibration, and light that are there for you. Allow the energy to enter your palms and move through your body.

Stay in this position for a minute, and then slowly lower your arms until you rest your hands palms up on your knees. Breathe and appreciate the energy within and around you. Take a few minutes and then slowly open your eyes.

- **See your light**. Do a round of *pranayama* or breath of fire breathing for about two minutes. If you haven't done this before, use the directions provided here and/or consult with someone experienced. Remove any glasses you might be wearing. Sit with the spine straight, heart open, and shoulders relaxed. Use the *maha-chin mudra* (index finger of each hand under the thumb), resting both hands palms up and fingers extended on both knees. This represents the Self superimposing itself over the ego. Breathing only through the nose, exhale strongly, pressing back on the abdomen and not moving the rest of the body. Allow the inhalations to happen by themselves. Begin slowly and steadily. Then breathe faster, and then breathe as fast as you can.

When you have finished the round, take the index and middle fingers of your left hand and place them horizontally over your left eye, and the same for your right hand and right eye, pressing gently though firmly. Hold them in position and see what you see, remembering to breathe. Do you see any light? This is who you are. At the same time, you can also place your left thumb in your left ear and your right thumb in your right ear. Press firmly. Do you hear anything?

- **Play with your energy**. After you've done *pranayama*, or after any breathing or meditation practice, with your eyes closed and hands resting open on your knees with palms up, move into your heart. Connect with the higher realms, your higher self, the Presence. Breathe and move this energy, this vibration, into your body through the brain and radiate it out throughout the physical form. Now focus your attention on your hands. Feel the energy and vibration moving into them.

Raise your hands very slowly, feeling the energy radiating from them. Move them around very gracefully, hands open and fingers extended. Continue to feel the energy and vibration emanating from your hands. After a few instants, face your hands toward each other about twelve inches apart without touching. See what you feel between your hands. Move them closer and farther apart slowly, noticing the difference. After a short while, place your hands just over any part of the body without touching. Create a relationship, and allow the energy to penetrate that part of the body for a minute. Finally, place your hands over your heart, slowly touching them to the heart. Breathe, and give thanks for the energy that you are now and always.

- **Manifest your intention.** We can use visualization and our energy to create opportunities and situations we'd like to happen in our lives. Think about an important meeting with another individual or a group that's coming up soon. Ask yourself what you'd like to see come from this meeting, what your intent is for the communication that will take place. Close your eyes and visualize your intent being fulfilled, what you and the person or people look like, what you're saying to one another, and what the outcomes are of your being together. Name different aspects of your intention to yourself, such as a certain agreement being made, a request or offer being accepted, something being created, a resolution of an issue, a greater relationship, teamwork, harmony, love, and/or unity between you and the other(s).

  While visualizing these aspects of your intention, breathe into your heart, and love and appreciate what you're seeing. Radiate this love from your heart to the person(s) present in this example, and be grateful for what's happening. Intensify this gratitude with your breath in your heart. Feel your energy expanding. Slowly open your eyes. When the actual meeting takes place, see how you feel during it. Debrief within yourself about the impact of your intention and visualization on what actually happened.

- **Embody your master.** If you have a spiritual master already in your life, call upon this person with all your heart. Feel deep gratitude for her service to you. Breathe the *Shakti*, the energy of this person into your entire physical body, down to the cells, and into your chakras and aura (subtle bodies). With your breath, establish and anchor this energy in you.

- **Manifest a master.** If you'd like to find a spiritual master to guide you in your path, call this person to you through your intent and ability to manifest. Take a few moments to access within yourself the qualities of the person, the feeling and energy you wish to feel in his presence. Declare that a master appear in your life with your breath, your heart, and your entire being. Feel gratitude for this manifestation in your life. In addition, speak to any others you know are engaged in a spiritual path. Discuss your vision, your intent for a master. Determine whether they know anyone who "fits the bill" or any sources of information you can pursue.

- **Use the Brain Illumination Method.** Sai Maa offers us different practices that activate our ability to transform and heal ourselves through the use of energy. *Brain Illumination Meditation* is a practice where we guide ourselves to bring light into our brain and physical and subtle bodies. (See www.sai-maa.com for more information.)

# WITH OTHERS:

- **Transform group energy.** We can transform not only our own energy but also that of others, including the people we live with, teams we're members of, and/or a community group. Notice the different interactions you have with others. Experiment and play with the energy to see what effect you have. Notice the group dynamics during your communication or interaction. Is the energy flowing, harmonious, and balanced, or is it disrupted or distorted? Are there peaks and valleys in the energy, from excitement and fast pace to peace or sluggishness? Are there different energies between specific individuals, with body language reflecting emotions or relationships that aren't loving or constructive?

  Through your awareness, be an active creator. Communicate energetically with your vibration, through the words you use, your body language, your intent, and your thoughts about the new energies you'd like to see manifested. Continue to focus on your own and the others' energies throughout the interaction. Reflect about what you've learned when it's over. Find other occasions when you can practice this, and notice the results.

- **Choose the energies you're in.** You can make decisions about certain individuals and groups to interact with, or not, in order to affect your energy field and subsequent transformation. Think about the energy (high or low, expanded or contracted, stable or scattered, loving or fearful) in your relationships, in certain groups, communities, places, and locations. By becoming aware of these energies and energetic patterns and by choosing the type and level of energy you want to be in, you can make life choices that bring you greater transformation.

- **Don't be affected by energies.** Think about whether there's energy coming from anyone you're with that you don't want to take on yourself. It's never about protecting yourself. As Maa says, protection comes from fear. However, you can avoid being affected by others' energies when you radiate like a bright sun, move into your heart and love, align with your Self, and spread your light. Practice this when you're with the person or individuals you identified. Shine like a sun. You can also visualize a thick layer of bright, white light around you that is open at the top and bottom so that the Earth and cosmic energy feed you. You can say to yourself, "I am light" or "Christ light!"

- **Practice Sai Maa Diksha**: Sai Maa offers us practices that enable us to serve others for self-healing. *Sai Maa Diksha* is an initiation of light into the brain of those receiving diksha. The light moves through and around the body and activates their personal healing field of energy. (See www.sai-maa.com for more information.)

# THOUGHTS

(Gaining new awareness for action, shifting and transforming thoughts)

- **Think in the body.** All thoughts are energy. When we think, most if not all our thoughts aren't inside the body; they're outside, in front of the body. This is why they can take over. We sometimes call this the monkey mind. One practice to master the mind is to choose one thought and bring it into the body with the breath. Feel it in a specific location in the body such as your throat or chest. Continue to breathe. Focus the thought in the body, and see what happens to the thought. See if it disappears, or if you have more power to transform it or act on it.

- **Move thoughts from the mind to the heart.** What we call negative thoughts come from the ego that wishes to keep us separate and unaware of our true Self. These traps catch us in our mind and affect our thoughts, as well as associated emotions. We're uncomfortable and many times not conscious of what's causing our discomfort and suffering. Here are some examples of where you may wish to focus and transform your thoughts: judgment of yourself or others, doubt, avoiding responsibility, distractions (by desires, senses, addictions, attachments), explanation and justification, arrogance.

  Try this practice. Imagine that you're bringing each negative thought down through two channels or tubes of light from the base of each ear on either side of the neck into the heart. Bringing the thought into the heart will help merge the energy of the thought with the energy of love that is always in the heart.

- **Stick out your tongue.** An easy way to stop the mind is to put the tongue out—way out. When you stick out your tongue all the way, your thoughts slow down and stop, you can't think.

- **Reduce your processing time.** Reflect about how often and how long you analyze and process before you decide and act. Choose one example and move forward more quickly than is your pattern. Take another example; take as many as you can.

- **Create a powerful context for yourself.** Reflect about your life right now. Identify whether there's a major shift, change, or transition going on. If there is, determine whether you have a good sense about how it fits with you. For example, determine whether it fits with the rest of your life, with who you are now or want to be in the future, and with a vision or intention you have for your life. See what context you have for what's happening. See whether you need to shift it to be more powerful or effective.

  If you, in fact, feel positive and powerful, and there's no change to be made in how you see the situation, just state and appreciate the context you have silently to yourself, such as, "On the job, I'm an even fuller expression of what I love to do." On the other hand, if you feel uncomfortable and ineffective, see how you can shift the context by creating a new *declaration* for yourself. A declaration is a certain type of linguistic expression through which we invent a future for ourselves that wasn't there before. The declaration brings into life a future that we can live into in the present, a transformation, a shift in being. This statement can began with "I declare I ..." or "I commit to ..." or "I (active verb) ...." Some examples are: "I commit to speak my truth powerfully at all times and in all circumstances," or "I seize all opportunities to be fully expressed and creative in my life." Come up with the declaration, write it down, and repeat it to yourself several times. See what happens in how you view the situation, the decisions and actions you can take. Express this declaration in action.

- **Reflect about recurrences in your life.** Think about people, places, situations, and opportunities in your life. Mark down in your journal or on paper whether any of these have reappeared at different points in time. If any have, focus on each one you've identified. Just sit with it, feel deep down whatever you feel. Then think about whether there's a reason for this. What can you learn from it? What is being said to you through this? Determine whether there's any action to take beyond your being more aware.

- **Identify patterns in your timeline.** Be more specific by drawing a timeline of your life along the top of several pieces of paper with five- or ten-year increments (e.g., 1950–1955 or 1950–1960). Under each column, write down the most significant people you met, situations you experienced, events that occurred, or major opportunities when you expressed yourself. When you're done, take a look across all the columns and see if there are any patterns, if any are repeated in more than one increment. What can you learn from taking a broad view of the whole timeline and looking at specific recurrences within it? Again, are there any actions for you to take now?

- **Drop expectations.** Whenever you have high expectations for yourself or projects or activities you're involved in, see whether you're pushing yourself too hard. See if you're focusing solely on the outcomes and results rather than being present with how you're acting or being. Perhaps you're getting down on yourself for not meeting your expectations or having too many of them. Make any necessary adjustments to reduce your self-judgment or disappointment with yourself.

- **Shift your relationship with making mistakes.** Witness what happens when you make a mistake, the thoughts that occur to you about yourself and the situation. Notice whether you judge or blame yourself or others. Realize that learning can't happen without admitting your mistakes, without seeing yourself as a beginner and accepting that you don't know something. Find ways to care for yourself by transforming your thoughts and feelings as soon as they arise.

- **Master your focus.** Determine whether you're paying attention to something or someone, focusing there, and creating discomfort or unwanted feelings within yourself due to this focus. This can be in the realm of relationships, exercise and health, your work life, or something else. Practice changing your focus, holding your attention elsewhere, so that you move into a new and more satisfying state. Consider using your breath and any practices or tools that will refocus your attention (e.g., meditation, mantras).

- **Unattach yourself.** Make a list of things or people you are attached to. This means people you're afraid of losing, you're holding onto, you're relying upon to feel better about yourself and your life, you're defining yourself by, and so on. Choose one attachment to experiment with. Close your eyes and picture the person or thing gone, disappeared, out of your life. How does this feel? What thoughts come to you? Write these down, and see what you learn about yourself. Shift your thoughts, your perspective about the person or thing. See if you can have a conversation that will serve you to unattach yourself. Here's another practice to try with your attachment: See the person less often, or remove the thing from your home or everyday life. See what happens inside you. Come up with other ideas for loosening the grip of the person or thing in your life.

- **Stop resisting.** Take stock of what you're resisting in your life, where you feel you're not in the flow. Identify the consequences and costs of this resistance. Identify the benefits and payoffs of shifting it. List and carry out any actions within yourself or with others to make the shift and move with the current.

- **Review lost opportunities.** Have you regretted not experiencing something that you might have, participating in some event, or meeting some person? Think back to how you might have hesitated or procrastinated. Ask yourself why this might have been. See what you learn about yourself. Can you apply anything you've learned to your present life and decisions about yourself, others, or situations?

- **Reduce and benefit from your fantasy life.** You don't necessarily have to eliminate all your fantasies. Just see whether there are any you're particularly attached to that influence how present you are in your life with your partner, in close relationships, and in pursuing and attracting new relationships. Identify the qualities of the other person or yourself that are present in your fantasies. See whether they'll actually serve you in your "real" life. If yes, make a note of these qualities and create an intention to attract them into your life or to develop them, along with any other qualities. If you have a partner, identify how she already possesses these qualities, and appreciate them. Activate them through your relationship. The same for yourself. If your partner doesn't have these qualities, determine whether you feel it's possible for him to develop them or if you should express them in the relationship yourself. Use your fantasies to build your current or future relationship. Don't use them to distract yourself from your relationship or to diminish opportunities that are available in it.

# EMOTIONS AND FEARS

(Releasing and transforming them)

- **Transform the emotion by bringing it to your heart.** Visualize a situation or a person where you have a very strong emotion that's you'd like to transform, perhaps something that you're very afraid of in your life. Put yourself internally in the midst of this fearful situation. Breathe and relax the body. Where do you feel the emotion or fear in the body? Breathe into that area. Many of the negative emotions rest in the gut, stomach area, or solar plexus. This is also the location of what we call the "karmic bag" that holds old patterns and memories from this and other life experiences. After you locate the emotion, move your hands to where you feel it in the body. Cup your hands under it. Breathing naturally, move your hands slowly up the body, holding the emotion until you reach your heart. Feel the love within you spread from the heart, enveloping the emotion as it disappears.

- **Transform the emotion by spreading light within it.** One way to transform the emotion is to focus and find a small spark of light within the area where you feel the emotion. Breathe into it and ask or command the light to expand. Love and embrace this light, allowing it to grow brighter and brighter with each breath. After a short period of time, you'll notice that the emotion has disappeared into light.

- **Use the release method.** We can release our emotions. They may include different fears, anger, frustration, resentment, nervousness, and anxiety. Use the following practice to release one particular emotion. Repeat the practice whenever you're feeling a strong emotion that you can't shift within yourself.

  Picture a difficult situation or issue that you face, or how you react to a certain person in your life. Feel the emotion associated with this situation or person. Allow yourself to feel it fully. These emotions are normally located in the belly. Be aware of this emotion as energy that wishes to be released and free, and is trapped because you're holding onto it.

  Bring your head down, moving your chin toward your collarbone. This movement disengages your mind. Breathe in and create an opening or gateway in your upper chest or heart area. Breathing again, bring the emotion and corresponding energy up from your belly to this gateway in your upper chest. With a strong exhale release the energy through the gateway and out through the front of your body. Breathe again and feel the difference. What you do feel? Do you still have the strong emotion toward the person or situation? If yes, practice the exercise again. If no, appreciate the transformation within yourself and move on.

- **Transform the triggers.** Choose one person or situation triggering you right now. Visualize what happens with this person or in this situation, meaning what happens inside you and in your actions and interactions. Be honest with yourself, and see what you're contributing to this situation. What are any thoughts, feelings, perspectives, or patterns that you need to transform? Once you identify any area within yourself to change, write it down. Specify any action steps for making that transformation. Use your plan to actually take action with the other person or in that situation. Acknowledge the results of your action.

- **Be a witness to your reactions and emotions**. Practice observing your emotions and reactions rather than getting stuck in them, being mastered by them. Choose one frequent reaction you have and experiment with it. For example, when you get frustrated with a certain person or situation or when you are upset with your partner for a certain behavior you perceive. See whether you can be aware of what comes up in you with this person or in this situation, and master the reaction before it happens. Or learn from it afterward so you can be more aware and less reactive the next time. See what happens with this practice, and then move on to another reaction and emotion to experiment with so you become more of an observer and witness.

- **Stop criticizing yourself.** See if there's any situation that gets you down about yourself or that you beat yourself up about. Reflect about this. Feel the consequences related to your body, relationships, and expression in life. Look at any standards you use to evaluate yourself. Are they too high, unattainable? See if you can adjust them. If you're angry, transform the anger. Transform any associated thoughts. If it applies, have a conversation that will bring you some clarity about your self-judgment and what you can do about it.

- **Face and transform your worries**. Choose one thing that you worry about regularly in your daily life. Reflect about this, and see what you can learn about the fear that underlies this worry. Is it about failing, being rejected, not being admired or loved, being seen as a fool? Stay with whatever you find out that underlies the worry, and truly feel what this feels like. Realize you're the one creating this within yourself, not the other people or the circumstances. Think about what you can do to face this worry and fear. Just like when I got into the inner tube, take action, and see what happens. Debrief within yourself. Don't stop there. Face it again in another way, at another time. Keep on practicing and moving through your worries and fears.

- **Eliminate doubt.** Find within yourself one area of life where you have great doubt (about yourself, another person, a situation). What does this feel like? What's your experience? Notice any judgments you have that are associated with this doubt, and distinguish your stories from the facts. Look to see if there is any pattern related to trusting others in your life. Uncover any fears. See if you can communicate or take explicit action with others to address this doubt.

# SELF-EXPRESSION

(Communicating and expressing yourself in new ways, a new way of being)

- **Shift from automatic to authentic listening**. When we're listening automatically, we're giving attention to the stories, interpretations, judgments, and running tapes about someone in our life. We're focusing on the noise or the nonstop words that are on repeat, such as, "I'm right, and you're wrong," "I agree," "I disagree," "That's true," "That's false," "I'm busy; what's your point?" or "What's in this for me?" Realizing this, choose a person and practice listening authentically. Find a case where there's something that the person wants to share and resolve with you. During the interaction, be completely present with the person. Determine whether thoughts are getting in the way, and decide to let them go. Turn down the volume. Put them aside, so you're open to listen fully to the person. See what happens that wouldn't have happened before in your interaction. Debrief within yourself and, if you choose, with the other person.

- **Practice authentic expression**. Choose an example where you're holding back from expressing yourself to someone due to how you may be seen, out of fear of not being liked, out of wanting to be seen positively. Know that not being authentic is affecting how you live your life and interact with others. Your inauthenticity is limiting the relationships you develop and the results you achieve. Have a conversation with the person you chose. Say first that you haven't been authentic. Then share your thinking, feelings, or opinions while asking the other person to listen. Notice how you're feeling and what you're thinking during the conversation. Transform whatever is necessary within you to be as fully open and authentic as possible. See what the two of you can create together based on this renewal of authenticity in your relationship.

  If it's not possible to have a conversation, write a letter to the person. Be honest about how you haven't been honest. Mention that you're writing for the sake of the relationship you wish to have with the person, or what you'd like to create together, or whatever benefits you see. You may also write a letter to someone with whom you no longer have contact to express yourself authentically for completion. This can include people who have left the body.

- **Express devotion.** Find within yourself one area of your life where you feel you're truly devoted, for example, to a person, activity, or teaching. What does this feel like? What's the experience for you? Magnify this feeling and experience through your imagination, and rest in this for several moments. Determine what new actions you will take to express your devotion even more.

- **Be your truth.** Find an area in your life where you're not being honest, authentic, and standing in your truth. Reflect on why this is so. Determine what action you will take to transform this, to express and live your truth. Take whatever action is required to make the shift. This is as easy as making a decision to act. At the same time, remember about discernment in your actions and compassion in your interactions (love with understanding).

- **Speak up.** This is another opportunity for authentic expression, in this case speaking a truth for you that you didn't express before. This may mean speaking to someone who did something you didn't agree with or like. It may be someone who reacted to another's actions in a way you didn't agree with. Choose an example that's centered around a fundamental truth that you value in life, something you feel strongly about.

  In preparing your conversation, remember to start first with the importance of the relationship, or the benefits of the conversation from your perspective. First ask the person to listen so you can express yourself, and then he can respond afterward. Remember to speak honestly. When the other person speaks, remember to listen authentically. See how you feel at the end of the conversation. Are there any follow-up actions to take? What's the state of the relationship if there is one going forward? What did you learn about yourself for future opportunities to speak up?

- **Go with what feels right.** Speak to a person. Pursue an activity. Join a group or community where you feel a natural attraction. I'm not speaking about physical or sexual attraction. This kind of attraction is a resonance or comfortable feeling deep within yourself. Decide to make a phone call, send a text or e-mail message, or attend a meeting. Just go for it. Be present with what occurs within you and with the other person or people. Reflect about what you thought would happen and what actually happened. Continue to take these kinds of steps aligned with what you feel deep down. Pick up on the cues and signals that we often ignore or don't pursue.

- **Say yes more often.** Especially in cases where you normally say no to yourself or others, play with saying yes, and see what happens. Do you overcome some fear? Do you learn something you couldn't have learned otherwise? Do you meet people or get to know people better than before? Do your shift your mood from pessimistic to optimistic, or reactive to proactive? Choose people you know, groups you are part of, and play with saying yes to them. Expand your yeses throughout different parts of your life. Ask others if they see a difference in you without mentioning that you're saying yes more often. Take in their feedback, and play some more.

- **Seek alignment through life changes.** See whether there are areas of your life that don't feel aligned with your current state, energy, values, interests, knowledge, or skills. Determine what life choices you will make, with the related action steps and time frames, so that you have people, work, and pursuits that fulfill you. Don't be rash; use your discernment and act. Explore, experiment, and be courageous.

- **We're creators, so create.** As creators, we can reinvent our lives and ourselves. We have the power and responsibility to eliminate the suffering we create in our lives, to create divine lives in which we live as the Self. We can take action to express our gifts and passions more freely.

Choose one thing you'd like to create in your life right now. What comes to you when you think about it? Do you feel willing and passionate, or passive and powerless? Reflect and identify exactly what you'd like to create. Name specific aspects of this creation to yourself. The greater the specificity and clarity, the greater the likelihood that you'll create what you're looking for. Now think about the possible actions you can take to achieve what you've identified. Weigh these possible actions in terms of their impact on creating what you'd like. Choose one or more actions that resonate and have the greatest impact. Now take action to create what you'd like. As you do, keep in your mind and heart those aspects of the creation you've identified. Feel how important they are to you, how you'd like to see them in your life. Reflect about your progress. Make any necessary adjustments, and keep going until you've created everything you imagined.

- **Apply lessons.** In recognizing what you've learned recently about yourself, see where you will apply lessons more than you already have. Incorporate insights into your work setting and with family members and friends, so that you're interacting and communicating in new ways. See what else you still need to learn to express yourself more effectively and powerfully in life.

- **Simplify.** Choose an area of your life, including any projects you're involved in or actions you're taking, that feel complicated or heavy to you. This might also be your overall schedule if it is packed with activities. Take time to see what you can simplify. Identify your priorities. Eliminate what doesn't matter as much or what doesn't serve you. Put the word "simplify" on a piece of paper or a magnetized board. Place it on your refrigerator, desk, or in a prominent location so you'll see it often.

- **Serve however you can.** Notice where you're serving now in your life. This means you don't have expectations for what you'll receive in return for what you're doing. Determine whether you can serve more. This can be through specific actions, projects or programs with individuals, groups, or communities. Choose one service activity or project you can engage in immediately, and take action. This doesn't have to be monumental or long-term in duration. As you're serving and when you've completed your activity, take note of how you feel. What's shifted within you? How have others responded? Be grateful for this opportunity to serve.

- **Experiment with your feminine side.** Reflect about what's more masculine or feminine within you and how you feel about this. Discuss with those whose opinion you value what is meant by the divine feminine. See how what you find out relates to you, your state, your perspective about yourself and the world, what you value in life, and your behaviors and actions. Make decisions and take actions that will activate and allow the divine feminine to be revealed in you and your life.

- **Balance your masculine and feminine sides.** I'm sure you know this isn't about being heterosexual or homosexual. It's about finding aspects within yourself and related behaviors and actions that are associated with masculine and feminine. Then it's about finding a happy balance between the two.

Take out some paper, or use your journal. Draw a line down the middle of two pages, creating two columns on each page. On one page write the title "Feminine," and on the other page write "Masculine." Using only the column on the left side of each page, write the *aspects* or *qualities* associated with feminine or masculine, and then in the right column of each page write the associated *behaviors* or *expressions* of these aspects/qualities. When you're done, take out a highlighter marker and mark those aspects/qualities and behaviors/expressions that you feel describe who you are right now. Then take a look to see what other aspects/qualities and associated behaviors/expressions you feel you can focus on in balancing your sides, so to speak.

Choose one quality and play with this in your life. Find examples at home, at work, with your partner, family, colleagues, and so on to develop and express it through your actual behaviors. Reflect about how you see yourself and others as you do this and when you debrief within yourself after the fact. Journal about what you find out. Have conversations with your partner, if there is one in your life, and with others who are important to you, about what you've learned. Keep on practicing, choosing new qualities and behaviors to develop.

- **Express yourself as a leader.** Look at yourself honestly. Distinguish the context in which you see yourself and your leadership, how you see yourself as a leader. Ask yourself, "In what areas of my life am I a leader or asked to be a leader? What criteria or measures do I use to assess my leadership? In other words, what's effective leadership for me?"

In writing, distinguish aspects of how you view your leadership that *empower* you in being an effective leader. Acknowledge and appreciate how you see yourself in these cases. Next, distinguish aspects of how you see your leadership that *limit* you in being an effective leader and that you'd like to transform. List these.

Determine what aspects inspire you, resonate in your heart, about being a leader. These are aspects you wish to embody and express in your life. Recalling the inner constraints you'd like to transform that limit you in being a leader, and what now inspires you, choose *one aspect* of yourself to transform in order to create a breakthrough in your leadership. Related to this aspect, visualize how you'd like to be acting and being as a leader.

A certain type of linguistic expression is called a *declaration*, through which we invent a future for ourselves that wasn't there before. The declaration brings into life a future that we can live into in the present, a transformation, a shift in being. This statement of declaration can begin with, "I declare I ..." or "I commit to ..." or "I (active verb) ..." Some examples are, "I commit to speak my truth powerfully at all times and in all circumstances," or "I seize all opportunities to be fully expressive and creative in my life."

For the breakthrough in your leadership and the aspect you choose to transform, make a new declaration to yourself for how you'll see yourself, how you'll act and be in the future. Write down *one declaration* that you'll commit to and practice. Come up with concrete examples of new thoughts you will have about yourself and new behaviors that reflect this declaration. Go out and practice your declaration. Notice and appreciate the results.

# RELATIONSHIPS

(Transforming relationships with family, friends, colleagues, community)

- **Communicate.** Reflect about whether you speak with your child enough. See whether you need to find more time to get together. This isn't to be a formal meeting; it should be a setting your child can enjoy. Aside from taking the step of scheduling time and creating new opportunities to communicate, determine how you'll speak and listen differently from how you have in the past. Remember about authentic expression and listening. Practice when you're together. Be open and honest. Ask questions and listen from where your child is coming from rather than from your own position.

- **Find ways to express your love and gratitude**. Feel what you love about your child. Think about how your child expresses herself or hi.,mself in unique ways, the special gifts or qualities your child possesses. Be spontaneous and find ways to honor your child in how you speak and what you say about him when the gift or quality is expressed. When you go to rest the body at night or get up in the morning, take a moment to be grateful that your child is in your life. Visualize your child, your relationship, your time together, and his impact on your life.

- **Check in.** Once in a while, ask your child how she is feeling about you and your relationship; ask whether anything can or should change and whether there are new ways you can be together. You might get some good feedback, although this may depend upon the age of your child. A teenager may just ignore the question. Say you're really interested in feedback and that you want to do whatever's possible to have the best relationship with your child.

- **Experiment with the keys to a divine relationship.** A divine relationship is typified by the relationship of gurus or masters who see no separation, who love each other as one soul. There are all assortments of human relationships, many of them limited by the perspective that we're separate from one another. We can develop divine relationships with a partner or loved one, although not many exist nowadays. More can exist, however, when we devote ourselves to looking inside, doing our practices, and transforming so that we're able to express ourselves in relationship as soul, as spirit.

Important keys to a divine relationship include the following verbs, meaning our behaviors and actions with a partner or loved one: respect, honor, appreciate, drop expectations, care, serve, rejoice, express all of you. Use these keys to a divine relationship with your partner and/or with other important relationships in your life. First, list the keys. For each, identify specific examples you can practice right now. Pay particular attention to joy (rejoice). Add other qualities and examples of divine relationship that come to you that you'd like to practice. Be aware and creative. Be courageous and outrageous. Be a divine lover however and whenever you can.

- **Show more of yourself.** Think about aspects of yourself you haven't expressed with your child, especially the more playful, freer, lighter parts of who you are. Choose one aspect and decide what you can do right now to express it. Set up the right time, right place, and best conditions for expressing it. Express, experiment, explore. Ask your child what she would like to see you express that you haven't shown before. Play with this. Have fun and be loose.

- **Do practices together in your relationship.** Identify spiritual or transformative practices you and your partner will do at the same time. Speak with one another honestly about your spiritual paths, whether you're in one or thinking about it. Identify together what you will pursue, co-create, and enjoy together. Some options? Meditate together. Go for walks in nature. Exercise or go to the spa. Eat together consciously. Attend gatherings or talks. Create an altar or meditation space you share. Read a book to each other, or read individually and then discuss what you've learned about qualities of relationship you'd like to develop. Take time to share and practice together to build and enrich your relationship.

- **Clean up your relationships.** Identify any relationships in which you're attached, in which you're dependent on the other person to complete you and fill you with what you feel is missing in yourself. See what needs to shift in each of these relationships. Communicate with the other person, stating what you feel and what you'd like—make specific requests. Set a new agreement for future interaction.

- **Express forgiveness.** Remember, the more you express your love for your child, the more you transform your relationship and the less anyone needs to forgive. If there are actual situations from the past for which you know your child really needs to forgive you and you need to ask for forgiveness, use the following practice—if you feel it's appropriate and the right time.

Say to your child that you know something is bothering her, or bothering you, and you'd like to speak about it. Ask your child if she accepts to speak about this. If no, then it's not the right time, so don't force it. If yes, then start with how important your relationship is to you, how much you love your child. Bring up the situation, your feelings about both what happened and your relationship, and ask for forgiveness. Next listen to what she has to say. Demonstrate authentic listening without interrupting to explain, without letting the stories or judgments in your head get in the way. Say, "Yes, I hear you." Rather than saying, "I was wrong. I'm sorry," say, "I understand. I know

now, and I didn't know before. I love you, and it won't happen again," or something in this vein.

In terms of forgiving your child for some behavior, reaction, or words spoken, you can forgive him within yourself unless your child is much older and it serves you, your child, or your relationship to express your feelings and how you forgive him.

As for forgiving yourself, think about your actions, thoughts, or feelings in the situation. Accept that you made a mistake. See what you learned from it, and realize how the relationship has evolved through it. Acknowledge your role. Take responsibility, be kind to yourself, and move on.

- **Create more community.** Identify how you will come together more with others or engage more in your existing communities. Express yourself more in these settings. Encourage everyone to share about his personal growth and transformation and for all members to take action together that will serve the group or community.

- **Build community support for your practice.** If you're already in a community or supported by others, reflect about the benefits of being together. Identify any actions you'd like to take to have this support be even more powerful. Take those actions. If you're not part of a community or supported by others, determine what steps you'll take, conversations you'll have, to become a member of a community or to receive support from loved ones, acquaintances, or those you don't yet know. You may choose to go to the HIU website and identify a nearby Sai Maa Center where you'll attend regular meditations and *satsangs*. See if any Sai Maa Diksha training is taking place near you, and attend the training.

# HEALTH

(Being more aware of and strengthening your health)

- **Get informed.** Information helps us to determine where to focus in improving our health and how this we will do this. We can learn more about the body and our anatomy, including: the functions of different organs and glands, or the endocrine system; the workings of other internal systems such as respiratory, digestive, circulatory, urinary; the parts and operations of the brain and nervous system; information about the skeletal and muscular systems; the five senses; the functioning of the cells, molecules, atoms, and the sub-atomic level.

We can research the subtle energy channels and bodies (chakras, *nadis,* meridians, *marmas,* interconnected layers of our aura). We can learn about the relationships between the physical and subtle, for example, how our physicality is affected by the state of our subtle bodies and what passes through them to the body.

Then there's information we can find within ourselves. This requires honesty. We're more likely to know what needs to transform when we're honest with ourselves. For example, when we face what's unhealthy about ourselves and our choices (e.g., smoking, excess drinking or eating, too much sugar, no exercise, pushing ourselves with no rest). Once we know the health outcomes we'd like to achieve, we then identify steps to take by researching specific practices, tools, teachers and practitioners, and facilities available to us.

- **Relax in the body.** Stretch and breathe during the day. Be aware of where you have aches or pains, where you feel stiff, and breathe there. Move the body, whether you're standing or sitting, by exhaling and twisting your torso to look behind you to the left, then breathing and twisting to the right. Bend down and stretch your lower back. Sway your arms up and down at the sides of your body. Yawn with your mouth wide open. Sigh loudly a few times.

- **Read physical signs.** If you show any physical signs, such as recurring pains, injuries, or illnesses, take some time to reflect about what the body might be telling you. Pain in the neck or shoulders might indicate you are carrying some burden, or spending much of your time taking care of others. Clenching of your teeth and jaw problems might mean you are holding something in and not expressing yourself. Difficulty breathing, congestion, or trouble with your lungs might be a sign of sorrow, grief, abandonment, or some other deep hurt. Knee problems might mean difficulty giving in, being humble, or surrendering. Foot problems may show you're not grounded or in the body or that you wish to escape something. Don't overanalyze and make things significant. Just identify some signs, if there are any, and see what you're to transform about yourself. Take any necessary steps, including consulting with health care practitioners.

- **Exercise.** There are three types of exercises: flexibility and stretching exercises that improve the range of motion of muscles and joints, balance, agility, and coordination (yoga, Tai Chi, dance and movement); aerobic exercises (fast walking, running, swimming, biking) increasing cardiovascular endurance and muscle density; anaerobic exercises (weight machines and training, sprinting) increasing muscle mass and strength.

Other examples of exercise include: walking and hiking with conscious breathing, especially in nature; racketball and various sports (tennis, basketball, soccer); jumping on the trampoline, which stimulates the lymphatic system. During more strenuous exercise, it's essential to have a good diet to ensure the body has the correct ratio of macronutrients, and provides sufficient micronutrients that aid the body in recovery so it doesn't depend upon fat content for survival.

- **Get some "R & R" (rest and relaxation).** The body must rest and relax in general, and during or after daily activities that may cause mental, emotional, or physical stress. Of course, breathing is conducive to our relaxing and also releasing. Having a sufficient number of hours to rest the body at night is important for our rejuvenation. Other "R

& R" activities include going to a health club or spa to take sauna or steam and use a jacuzzi; different types of massage (e.g., deep tissue, Swedish); laying in the sun; going to hot springs if accessible.

In addition, we relax when we smile or laugh. This affects the parasympathetic system. Fortunately, we can do this anywhere and anytime, reflecting the impact of joy in our lives. We can release and be more relaxed as a consequence, by crying, screaming, and expressing ourselves, not holding down what needs to surface to be transformed. Singing our favorite songs relaxes us, as does chanting when we give ourselves to the chant that activates within us the energy of the deity whose name we are chanting. Chanting is useful for moving us into a state of meditation. Another way to relax is doing what we enjoy (interests, hobbies), such as gardening and working with nature.

- **Watch your diet and nutrition**. We could say we are what we eat, as the food we take into the body impacts our health and daily functioning. This includes the state of our stomach and strength of our digestive system, our ability to absorb nutrients, and what foods and dietary supplements improve our health and prevent disease and deterioration of the body.

  We can pay attention to our food combinations, where certain foods take different amounts of time to digest, or if taken together create fermentation. For example, it's best not to combine proteins (e.g., nuts, eggs, meats, seafood) with dairy, potato, or grains, which are carbohydrates and ferment protein, creating greater acidity in us. It's beneficial to avoid drinking fluids with meals, and to eat fruits alone or separated from meals by a certain amount of time. For optimal digestion, it's best to have smaller meals eaten slowly and to rest after eating. Gluten-free diets are best to avoid wheat allergy. Vegetarian diets include living food with nutrients present in vegetables. They're also free from the density of meat and, as some say, the fear present in the animal being killed.

  A very important consideration in our diet is the balance of acid and alkaline (pH) in the body. On a scale of 1–14 with lower being acidic and higher alkaline, 7.4 is an ideal balance for liquids in the body, including water, blood, lymph, and brain fluid. A result of high acidity is low oxygen in the cells, which leads to fermentation, oxidation, and oxidative stress, which affects the health of the cells. Our health is improved with less sugar, and with antioxidant rich, less acidic, and more alkaline fruits and vegetables. Some oils that are very beneficial in our diet include flax, hemp, coconut, and olive. Juices are very popular, and green drinks are highly beneficial to our health (e.g., wheatgrass), as well as shakes with low acid fruits.

- **Consider health care services**. The services offered by medical and health care practitioners preserve our well-being on all levels. They prevent, treat, and manage poor health, injuries. and disease. They include those services considered complementary or alternative that come from certain traditions, such as those in India and China. Seven such services include: chiropractic, osteopathy, craniosacral therapy, rolfing or structural integration, *Ayurveda*, homeopathy and acupuncture.

# APPENDIX 3
## *Read, Listen and Watch: Books, CDs and DVDs*

**Books**: Reading brings us new awareness and insights, practices and tools we can apply in our lives and for our transformations. I'm recommending below just some of my favorite books that I've read over the years with Maa. They're listed in very loose order of preference, except for the first book, which wins hands down.

*Petals of Grace: Essential Teachings for Self-Mastery.* H.H. Sai Maa Lakshmi Devi. Colorado: HIU Press, 2005.

*Life and Teachings of Mary and Jesus.* A.D.K. Luk. A.D.K. Luk Publications, 1983.

*Law of Life (Volumes 1 and 2).* A.D.K. Luk. A.D.K. Luk Publications, 1959, 1960.

*I Am Discourses.* Ascended Master Saint Germain. St. Germain Press, 1980.

*Unveiled Mysteries.* Godfre Ray King. St. Germain Press, 1989.

*Magic Presence.* Godfre Ray King. St. Germain Press, 1993.

*Autobiography of a Yogi.* Paramahansa Yogananda. Self-Realization Fellowship, 1998.

*Life and Teachings of the Masters of the Far East (6 volume set).* Baird T. Spaulding. Devorss & Company, 1986.

*I Remember Union: The Story of Mary Magdalena.* Flo Aeveia Magdalena. All Worlds Publishing, 1992.

*Anna, Grandmother of Jesus.* Claire Heartsong. S.E.E. Publishing Company, 2002.

*The Bhagavad Gita.* Maharishi Mahesh Yogi. Arkana Penguin Books, 1990.

*Paths to God: Living the Bhagavad Gita.* Ram Dass. Three Rivers Press, 2004.

*Be Here Now.* Ram Dass. Lama Foundation, 1971.

*Sai Baba Gita: The Way to Self-Realization and Liberation in this Age.* Compiled and edited by Al Drucker. Atma Press, 2000.

*Love All Serve All: A Pictorial Message of the Lord.* Sathya Sai Publications of New Zealand.

*The Disappearance of the Universe: Straight Talk about Illusions, Past Lives, Religion, Sex, Politics, and the Miracles of Forgiveness.* Gary Renard. Hay House, Inc., 2002.

*A Course in Miracles: Combined Volume.* Foundation for Inner Peace, 2007.

*The Book of Knowledge: The Keys of Enoch.* J.J. Hurtak. The Academy for Future Science, 1977.

*The Ancient Secret of the Flower of Life (Volume 1).* Drunvalo Melchizedek. Light Technology Publishing, 1990.

*Serpent of Light: The Movement of the Earth's Kundalini and the Rise of the Female Light 1949 to 2013.* Drunvalo Melchizedek. Weiser Books, 2007.

*Electrons: The Building Blocks of the Universe* by the Ascended Masters. Ascended Masters Teachings Foundation, 1995.

*Energy Blessings from the Stars: Seven Initiations.* Virginia Essene & Irving Feurst. Spiritunfold, 1998.

*Babaji and the 18 Siddha Kriya Yoga Tradition.* Marshall Govindan. Kriya Yoga Publications, 1991.

*The Mother.* Sri Aurobindo. Sri Aurobindo Ashram Trust, 1995.

*Love Without End: Jesus Speaks.* Glenda Green. Spiritis, 1998.

*The Illuminated Rumi.* Translations and commentary by Coleman Barks. Broadway Books, 1997.

*Sacred Mirrors: The Visionary Art of Alex Grey.* Inner Traditions International, 1990.

*The House of Belonging.* Poems by David Whyte. Many Rivers Press, 1992.

*The Biology of Belief: Unleashing the Power of Consciousness, Matter and Miracles.* Bruce Lipton. Mountain of Love/Elite Books, 2005.

*Practical Spirituality.* John Randolph Price. Hay House, Inc., 1985.

*The Three Laws of Performance: Rewriting the Future of Your Organization and Your Life.* Steve Zaffron & Dave Logan. Jossey-Bass, 2009.

**CDs and DVDs:** These can be used for chanting, dance, movement, exercise, meditation, relaxation, and learning new teachings and practices. The list isn't exhaustive. It includes those I've especially enjoyed, and provides you some focus and direction for further research. For more information about Sai Maa's offerings, please go to www.sai-maa.com.

- Selected Sai Maa CDs:

  Chanting—"Shma Israel."

Meditation—"Power of the Violet Cosmic Flame," "Silent Meditation," "Meditations for Daily Practice, Volume 1 & 2."

Teachings—"Love," "Ultimate Healing," "Divine Healing," "The Passion to Act," "The Soul of Relationships," "The Nobility of Women," "Creating Community," "The Intellectual Understanding of Enlightenment," "Path to the Luminous," "Sacred Teachings of the Masters," "Moving at the Speed of Love," "Know Yourself," "Kundalini: Sacred Healing Fire."

- Selected Sai Maa DVDs:

  "Brain Illumination," "Understanding Thought Forms, Entities and Karma," "A Dialogue with the Divine."

Other CDs

- "The Eternal Om," Valley of the Sun.

- Robert Gass—"Om Namah Shivaya," "Alleluia/Kyrie," "From the Goddess," "Medicine Wheel," "Hara Hara," "Kirtana." On Wings of Song.

- Krishna Das—"Pilgrim Heart," "Breath of the Heart," "One Track Heart."

- Snatam Kaur—"Grace," "Shanti," "Prem."

- Jai Uttal—"Kirtan: The Art and Practice of Ecstatic Chant," "Nectar."

- Paul Horn—"Inside the Great Pyramid."

- "Song of the Earth." Brain Mind Research Laboratories.

- David & Steve Gordon—"Sacred Earth Drums."

Other DVDs

- "Illuminated Chakras: A Visionary Voyage into Your Inner World.

## Paramacharya Swami Parameshwarananda (Swamiji) is the executive

director of Humanity In Unity (HIU), a nonprofit educational and humanitarian organization dedicated to global enlightenment. He is the resident spiritual master at the Temple of Consciousness ashram in Crestone, Colorado. Both HIU and the ashram were founded by Her Holiness Jagadguru Sai Maa Lakshmi Devi, an enlightened master and global humanitarian.

In his role as HIU executive director, Swamiji advises on numerous humanitarian projects, including those carried out in India in collaboration with the Sai Maa Vishnu Shakti Trust, founded by H. H. Sai Maa to plan and carry out humanitarian initiatives throughout India. The goal of most of these projects is to feed people. HIU has also provided financial and service support to the HIU-Vitamin Angels program "Healthy Children Strong India," that distributes anti-parasite medicine and vitamin A to children, with the intent of eliminating childhood blindness by the year 2020. Swamiji provides counsel for the construction of Sai Maa's ashram in Varanasi (Kashi), India, which will be the headquarters for humanitarian service managed by the trust.

In his leadership of HIU, Swamiji oversees educational and community activities encompassed within the Life Divine Initiative, a program that empowers an expanding international community to transform and serve the awakening of the planet (see _www.LifeDivineInitiative.com_). In addition to his spiritual leadership and service at the ashram, Swamiji teaches around the world and lectures at various international spiritual gatherings. He has published numerous articles about spirituality and personal and social transformation (available on the HIU website: _www.HumanityInUnity.org_).

Before moving in 2004 to the Crestone ashram, Swamiji lived for a year in India, focusing on his _sadhana_, which included his initiation as _brahmachari_ (monk). Prior to this, he lived for six years in the San Francisco Bay Area, where he was the local lead of the Sai Maa Center while also working as an organization consultant. His twenty-five-year consulting career included executive and employee coaching, organization, and leadership and team development, as well as leading an industry practice of consulting with Japanese and foreign-owned organizations. During that time, Swamiji was a partner with a major management consulting firm in New York and also started his own independent consulting practice, which included working with UNICEF on global management reform for several years. He received his PhD in organizational psychology and MS in psychology from New York University. He was a licensed psychologist in New York and also designated as Master Coach by a major international professional coaching association.

_**Please write Swamiji with any comments about the book at: Swamiji@HumanityInUnity.org.**_

15539943R00038

Made in the USA
Lexington, KY
03 June 2012